The Integrated Library

Encouraging
Access to
Multimedia
Materials

Second Edition
by Jean Weihs

Illustrated by Cameron Riddle

ORYX PRESS 1991

Copyright © 1991 by The Oryx Press
4041 North Central at Indian School Road
Phoenix, Arizona 85012-3397

Published simultaneously in Canada

Printed and Bound in the United States of America

∞ The paper used in this publication meets the minimum requirements of American National Standard for Information Science—Permanence of Paper for Printed Library Materials, ANSI Z39.48, 1984.

Library of Congress Cataloging-in-Publication Data

Weihs, Jean Riddle.
    The integrated library: encouraging access to multimedia materials / by Jean Weihs; illustrated by Cameron Riddle.
        p.   cm.
    Rev. ed. of: Accessible storage of nonbook materials. 1984.
    Includes bibliographical references (p. 127) and index.
    ISBN 0-89774-658-9
    1. Libraries—Special collections—Nonbook materials. 2. Shelving (for nonbook materials) 3. Libraries—Space utilization.
4. Library materials—Storage. I. Weihs, Jean Riddle. Accessible storage of nonbook materials. II. Title.
Z688.N6W42   1991
025.8´1—dc20   91-26027
                                                                    CIP

For Harry
Husband, Father
Friend and Editor

Contents

Preface

In 1967 I was faced with the task of cataloging the nonbook materials in all the schools in a borough of Metropolitan Toronto. I was undaunted because I have always believed that, if one can read, one can find the solutions to most problems. However, it soon became apparent that there was little to read on cataloging nonbook materials. In consulting people who had cataloged their nonbook collections, I found that they were unanimous about one point: the cataloging procedure each had used was not an effective tool for the retrieval of nonbook items in the collection. Eventually, after many discussions with librarians and media specialists who would either become my co-authors or participate in an advisory committee, we concluded that cataloging rules for all materials, both book and nonbook, should be based on the same principles so that all catalog records could be in one file. We also concluded that no such rules existed at that time.

Nonbook Materials: The Organization of Integrated Collections was written to fill that void. The investigation into the effective cataloging of nonbook materials for an active collection produced some interesting by-products; one of these was the realization that intershelving all or almost all materials in the collection in one classification sequence would lead to greater use of materials in circulating libraries. Two school librarians, one in an elementary school, the other in a junior high, had allowed us to rearrange their catalogs and collections to test our cataloging theories. We were delighted to find in both school libraries that the circulation of all materials rose when the collections were intershelved. Therefore, we added a small section on intershelving to our cataloging book.

Since that time I have participated in many workshops, seminars, and lectures on the organization of nonbook materials. Usually, during the discussion period, someone would raise a question about intershelving. I have also received many letters about storage methods. The first edition of this book, titled *Accessible Storage of Nonbook Materials*, was written in answer to those questions, and was received by librarians and media specialists with considerable interest.

In the intervening years libraries have reported that nonbook materials are the fastest growing parts of their collections. Many patrons have acquired VCRs, Walkmans, and microcomputers, and have overcome their original reluctance to handle equipment. This is reflected in an increasing demand for appropriate software, and a shift in emphasis from materials that were usually borrowed with equipment, e.g., 16-mm motion pictures, to media that can be used with home equipment, e.g., videocassettes. Growth is noted particularly in circulation statistics for videocassettes, followed by those for analog sound cassettes. Demand is increasing also for public domain microcomputer software.

The enhanced role of nonprint media in library collections, and the comments and suggestions of librarians and media specialists about the original work, have prompted this second edition. I am indebted to the many people who have taken the time to share their experience and knowledge with me. In particular, I wish to thank the staffs of the National Archives of Canada's Conservation Branch Moving Image, Data and Audio Conservation Division and Magnetic Media Division, and of the National Library of Canada's Preservation Office who willingly answered my questions. The chapter dealing with computer files was enriched by Ronald Weihs's vast knowledge of computers and computer software.

This book applies to collections that are directly accessible to the public where archival conservation plays little role. It is written for those who now intershelve part or all of their collections and are interested in learning of additional storage devices; for those who want to investigate the intershelving concept; and for staff in all open access libraries who are concerned about the proper care, handling, and storage of nonbook materials.

Few libraries have the resources to afford ideal conservation for all materials; they must do the best they can to circulate their materials while at the same time providing them with reasonable protection from damage. This book is a compilation of the opinions of experts and the practical experience of librarians. It presents a diversity of storage methods and devices available to libraries. A library may adopt some of them as useful to its needs, while discarding others as not pertinent to its objectives.

In response to suggestions that subject bibliographies would be more useful than the alphabetic arrangement adopted in the first edition, the citations on a particular topic are found at the end of the pertinent chapter. The General Bibliography at the end of this book contains citations in which subject content relates to more than one chapter. Citations from the first edition that have been repeated in this edition include those works considered by experts to be standard titles; information about "dying" media, such as analog sound discs, for which few new materials are being published; information about media, such as three-dimensional materials, where few works are written; and information about various topics where more recent information has not been found.

Introduction

After much research I have concluded that patron-oriented libraries should interfile all catalog records in one all-media catalog. Separate catalogs for each medium result in nonbook materials being used only by patrons who are knowledgeable about the library's catalogs and who are willing and have the time to search through them. In order for entries to be effectively interfiled, the same rules for descriptive cataloging and the same subject headings should be used for all materials. The *Anglo-American Cataloguing Rules*, second edition, 1988 revision (AACR2R),[1] is the standard for descriptive cataloging. *Sears List of Subject Headings* and *Library of Congress Subject Headings*[2] are the subject heading systems most commonly applied to general collections. Many subject heading lists have been devised for special collections.

An intershelved collection must be classified by a single classification scheme because items are shelved in one sequence. *Nonbook Materials: The Organization of Integrated Collections*[3] was written as a companion to AACR2R for libraries that list their collections in one catalog. It also discusses subject analysis for nonbook materials.

Intershelving is recommended for patron-oriented circulating libraries, i.e., school, public, community college, and some special libraries that do not have an archival function. Such libraries weed their collections of out-of-date or little used items. Their objective is a dynamic collection that can be easily browsed and retrieved by their public. The recommendations in this book about care, handling, and storage are those most feasible for a circulating library where preservation of materials is not the primary consideration.

The terms used for particular nonbook materials in this work are taken from AACR2R. The word "library" is meant to be synonymous with "resource center," "media center," "instructional materials center," "information center," etc.; "librarian" with "teacher-librarian," "media specialist," etc.; and "library staff" with all staff, whatever their official titles, in organizations that circulate nonbook materials.

This book discusses materials most commonly found in multimedia collections. Librarians who manage other types of media may find useful citations in the General Bibliography.

Illustrations showing methods of intershelving and storage devices do not always depict full shelves and containers because full shelves and containers may obliterate the point being illustrated.

Many books and articles are written about media. However, very little is published about what, in my opinion, are the two most important components of a dynamic multimedia library: the role of the staff and the interest of the patrons. Without the active support of both these groups, materials in the collection can become unused, expensive junk. Chapters 1 and 2 discuss the importance of staff and patrons and how intershelving can benefit them both.

Apologia for Intershelving Nonbook Materials

A youthful memory calls forth a small town library with books shelved by color and size by a librarian who prided herself on "tidy housekeeping": first, all red books filed shortest to tallest, then green books, blue books. . . . We may smile or shake our heads at this quaint storage method, but the "tidy housekeeper" mentality still has a foothold in the library world. Some librarians insist on the segregation of media because they claim that the shelves do not look attractive (i.e., "messy") when all materials are intershelved. Messiness may be the price to be paid for a dynamic collection. The main purpose of a library is not to present an aesthetic appearance but rather to make available the best and most useful material to the largest number of patrons—and intershelving will accomplish this. There are many, however, who would not agree that intershelving results in unattractive shelves, but they would argue that a variety of media shelved together creates an inviting appearance.

Intershelving is the logical arrangement for a browsing collection. All items on a particular subject are housed together, accessible and retrievable in a single search. This saves time for both patrons and staff because it eliminates the need to search in several places, reduces the number of directional questions a patron may have to ask, and generally eliminates the necessity of retrieving items from a storage area. Intershelving presents the entire range of materials on a given subject in a single location. If nonbook materials are shelved separately, patrons may fail to find useful items.

The discriminatory treatment of nonbook materials may deprive the patron of valuable information and/or enjoyment. If nonbook materials are stored in back rooms, poorly lighted corners, or out-of-the-way places, the patron will either be unaware of their existence or will assume that these materials do not have much value. Intershelving attests to the equal significance of all materials.

Intershelving may also introduce a new type of patron to the library—those people who have low reading skills and comprehend more effectively through sight or sound are particularly attracted to nonbook materials. The stigma attached to low reading skills is lessened when patrons use materials from the same shelves. Librarians have found that those who are generally nonreaders—for instance, some students scheduled into the school library—are attracted by items about their favorite hobbies. For example, a motorcycle enthusiast notices a study print on this subject and then examines the other items standing on the shelf—a videocassette, a filmstrip, a kit—and eventually reads the books on motorcycles. The desire to read these materials may be an impetus to improve reading skills.

Intershelving has helped teachers develop educational programs. They become more aware of the variety of materials available to meet the diverse needs of students and can direct particular students to nonbook materials.

Many librarians have reported that the introduction of intershelving greatly increased the circulation of *all* materials. In drawing attention to the variety of formats, intershelving leads to information from different perspectives and encourages its exploration. Some librarians were so impressed by the increased use of materials that they took their vertical file material out of filing cabinets and their subject-oriented periodicals off periodical shelves and housed them in pamphlet boxes, Princeton files, or boxes with the rest of the collection on the shelves. Their expectations were fulfilled—the materials were more widely used.

Open Access and Theft. Although, traditionally, hardware has not been considered part of a collection, some libraries have been so committed to optimum public service that they have placed their equipment on open access. Large pieces that will not circulate are bolted down if theft might be a problem. Smaller-sized equipment available for circulation is modified in some libraries to discourage theft. Items marked for circulation may be painted garish, unattractive colors and Sisterson describes "tape recorders screwed down on to large boards (approx. 18 inches square) which are still portable, but not too much so."[4]

The danger of theft and damage, foremost among the reasons cited for segregated storage, brings us to a discussion of the arguments raised against intershelving. It is argued that nonbook materials are expensive, easily damaged, and particularly subject to theft. The 1989 average price of a US hardcover nonfiction book was $42.97.[5] The 1989 prices of many media compare favorably with this; some nonbook items are expensive, but so are some books. Theft and damage should not, therefore, be more of a factor in the decision to provide open access for nonbook materials than it is for books.

During the 1970s and early 1980s many librarians with intershelved collections reported that damage and theft had not been major problems. This positive experience has continued to the present day.

> Over a five-year period our book losses averaged slightly under three percent yearly. In comparison, losses of non-book materials showed an average yearly loss as follows: phonodiscs—two percent, slides—two percent, tapes—two percent, transparencies—three percent, film loops— one percent, and filmstrips—one percent. During these five years there were no guards at the doors or any other forms of security.[6]

> The problem of easily damaged materials such as record albums can be minimized by either repackaging the resources in sturdier containers or reinforcing the covers of the present containers. . . . In the six years Lord Elgin has been open only one record album has been damaged because of this shelving method. (Stoness, Lord Elgin Secondary School)[7]

> 7 of the 22 centers conducted . . . research concerning the impact of integrating their media on bookshelves. The research generally consisted of conducting individual background studies prior to the decision to integrate the media. Also, some research was done after the system was in effect for a length of time to determine the extent of vandalism and materials loss. Little difference in the amount of vandalism and materials loss was found with the integrated shelving system. (Hart reporting on a survey of media centers across the United States)[8]

> The results of intershelving so far have been that student use of the materials has greatly increased, and their comments have been very favorable. . . . Only a few losses of materials have been sustained, and there has been a minimal amount of materials found in the wrong kits. (Wilson, Windward Community College)[9]

> That a majority of the respondents expressed that 'no noticeable difference' had occurred in the amount of theft or damage to nonprint materials is most encouraging. While overall library incidences of theft and damage go unabated, at least the concept of open shelving inherent in multimedia integrated shelving has not demonstrably contributed to the loss or mutilation of nonprint materials at the libraries surveyed. (Donnelly reporting on a survey question answered by 26 southeastern United States academic libraries)[10]

> One New York state public library director with a sizeable collection came to the conclusion that his shrinkage on an open stack approach would cost less dollars than paying staff to open and close cases. He found that not only was his loss experience extremely low, but also that his circulation tripled as patrons "paw through" the collection. (Short describing the benefits of open shelf video collections)[11]

> Software damage and theft has not been a problem. (Berglund reporting on the circulation of microcomputer software in a school library)[12]

> Libraries with open access seem generally to have suffered very small stock losses (a much lower percentage than for books, it should be noted). (Bryant describing the experience in British libraries)[13]

Several librarians commented that use of materials is discouraged when patrons are treated as potential thieves. Others believe that obvious measures taken to prevent theft are a challenge to the young.

It is clear that attitudes toward public property dictate the amount of theft and damage a library may experience. Both books and nonbook materials will suffer when the library serves patrons who consider theft and vandalism to be acceptable actions. A discussion of societal attitudes toward public property is outside the scope of this book. If a library is subject to this situation, a security system may solve the problem. Most systems can be adapted to various media or a system can be purchased specifically to deal with a particular problem.

> Using a videotape security system that operates on radio frequencies has almost eliminated theft in one library. Their collection is self service; "people can load up with videotapes, walk around all they like, but if they try to leave without checking them out, an alarm goes off." And there is no danger to the tapes themselves. (Avallone in a survey of the use of sound cassettes and videocassettes in libraries)[14]

If a library does not have a security system or their system cannot be adapted for use with some nonbook materials, it is still possible to achieve some reduction of theft and damage to these materials. Since the majority of nonbook items are nonfiction, placing nonfiction shelves as close as possible to the circulation desk or any other area where there is supervision assures constant surveillance. This is particularly effective in a small library. Furthermore, if there is a "run" on a particular medium, dummies or empty containers can be intershelved and the items kept at the circulation desk. The surrogate should have a description of the item or, at the very least, a copy of the catalog record attached to it.

Space for Special Materials. Some critics of intershelving claim that nonbook materials take up too much space on the shelves. Implicit in this remark is the idea that nonbook materials are not as worthwhile as books. If this were the case, it is debatable whether they were worth their purchase price in the first place.

Both books and nonbook materials range in size. Special shelving is made to accommodate oversize books; nonbook materials should be treated in the same manner. Many nonbook materials have containers similar in size to the book collection and are easily intershelved. Media too large for regular shelving should be intershelved in the oversize section.

Storage equipment designed for a particular medium, e.g., a microfilm cabinet, uses valuable space. Some librarians believe that intershelving a collection saves space because more shelving can be built in the places that used to have specialized equipment. Miller notes "when material is stored in pamphlet boxes on book stacks, it consumes less floor space than if it were housed in filing cases. Furthermore, extra space must be allowed in planning library quarters for the opening of file drawers."[15] During a three-month period in 1985 a public library in the Metropolitan Toronto area did a pilot study in three of their branches to determine the effect of placing analog sound cassettes on open access shelves. At the end of the study open access shelving was adopted by all branches because the loss rate had been low, much staff time had been saved, and the space previously occupied by cassette storage could be put to other uses.

Some libraries have small collections of local history and/or items unique to the institution. These may need archival preservation. Some citations found in Further Reading at the end of chapters or in the General Bibliography deal with the care, handling, and storage of archival materials. If it is possible to duplicate these materials without damaging them, the duplicated copies can be shelved with the regular collection. A description of the more fragile items can also be placed in a pamphlet binder and intershelved. In this way the total collection is readily available to the public.

On the other hand, the amount of time expended on cleaning, cataloging, and/or processing ephemeral materials should not exceed their value to the library. Items of temporary worth can be housed "as is" in a container labelled with a general classification number and shelved at the end of the classification sequence to which they pertain.

In sum, intershelving will make a library truly successful in a way in which success is measured in a library—it will make more materials readily accessible to a larger number of people. But making intershelving work requires the enthusiastic support of staff.

References

1. *Anglo-American Cataloguing Rules*, prepared under the direction of the Joint Steering Committee for Revision of AACR . . ., edited by Michael Gorman and Paul W. Winkler. 2nd ed., 1988 revision (Chicago: American Library Association; Ottawa: Canadian Library Association; London: The Library Association, 1988).

2. Both these subject heading systems are updated, LCSH more frequently than Sears. The latest editions should be used for the most effective subject retrieval.

3. Jean Weihs with assistance from Shirley Lewis, *Nonbook Materials: The Organization of Integrated Collections*. 3rd ed. (Ottawa: Canadian Library Association, 1989).

4. Joyce Sisterson, Jan Storey, Ian Winkworth, "Letters—Audiovisual Integration," *Audiovisual Librarian*, vol. 7, no. 1 (Winter 1981): 20.

5. *Bowker Annual Library and Trade Almanac*. 35th ed., 1990-91 (New York: Bowker, 1990), p. 508. This figure was calculated from prices given for all categories with the exception of fiction and juveniles.

6. Robert A. Veihman, "Some Thoughts on Intershelving," In *Planning and Operating Media Centers*. Readings from Audiovisual Instruction, 2 (Washington, DC: Association for Educational Communications and Technology, 1975), p. 38.

7. Jean Stoness, "Integration of Print and Non-Print Resources," *Expression*, vol. 1, no. 1 (Spring 1976): 36.

8. Thomas L. Hart, "Dare to Integrate," *Audiovisual Instruction*, vol. 21, no. 8 (October 1976): 18.

9. De Etta Wilson, "On the Way to Intershelving: Elements in the Decision," *Hawaii Library Association Journal*, vol. 33 (1976): 48.

10. Arthur R. Donnelly, "Multimedia Integrated Shelving: A Survey of Its Use in Academic Libraries of the Southwest with Guidelines for Implementation." Ed Diss., George Peabody College for Teachers, 1978 (Ann Arbor, MI: University Microfilms, 1979), p. 51.

11. Jack Short, "Video in the Collection," *Collection Management*, vol. 7, nos. 3/4 (Fall 1985/Winter 1985-86): 242.

12. Patricia Berglund, "School Library Technology," *Wilson Library Bulletin*, vol. 60, no. 6 (February 1986): 40.

13. E.T. Bryant with the assistance of Guy A. Marco, *Music Librarianship: A Practical Guide.* 2nd ed. (Metuchen, NJ: Scarecrow, 1985), p. 307.

14. Susan Avallone and Bette-Lee Fox, "A Commitment to Cassettes," *Library Journal*, vol. 111, no. 19 (November 15, 1986): 37.

15. Shirley Miller, *The Vertical File and Its Satellites: A Handbook of Acquisition, Processing, and Organization.* 2nd ed. Library Science Text Series (Littleton, CO: Libraries Unlimited, 1979), p. 48.

Further Reading

Association of College and Research Libraries. Audiovisual Committee. "Guidelines for Audiovisual Services in Academic Libraries." *College & Research Library News.* 48 (9) (October 1987): 533–36.

Dewing, Martha, ed. *Home Video in Libraries: How Libraries Buy and Circulate Prerecorded Home Video.* Professional Librarian Series. Boston: G.K. Hall, 1988.
    Based on a survey of over 900 public libraries with video collections, this book provides statistics about the theft of videotapes. "96.6% reported that their tape loss rate is not worse than the loss rate for books."

Fast Forward: Libraries and the Video Revolution, produced by Library Video Network. Chicago: ALA Video, 1988. Videocassette (VHS, Beta, or ¾ inch)
    An overview of videocassette use in U.S. public libraries.

Funk, Grace E. "Where Do I Look for It? On the Mechanics of the Integrated Collection." *Bookmark.* 16 (5) (January 1975): 13–17.
    Practical suggestions for intershelving.

Gandert, Slade Richard. *Protecting Your Collection: A Handbook, Survey, and Guide for the Security of Rare Books, Manuscripts, Archives, and Works of Art.* Library and Archival Security, vol. 4, no. 1–2. New York: Haworth Press, 1982.
    Illustrated by some humorous true tales, the author discusses the many threats to library collections, such as theft, fire, and mutilation, and the ways these may be avoided or ameliorated.

Hampshire, John A. "Putting Audiovisuals on the Shelf." *The Book Report.* 4 (5) (March/ April 1986): 21.
    A school librarian reports very positively on the intershelving of materials.

Hart, Thomas L., ed. "Integrated Shelving of Multimedia Collections." *School Media Quarterly.* 5 (1) (Fall 1976): 19–30.
    Four librarians discuss their positive experiences with intershelving.

Heery, Michael J. *Audiovisual Materials in Academic Libraries.* Wigston, Leicester: Library Association Audiovisual Group, 1984.
    This report on the extent of AV librarianship and the value of AV materials in British academic libraries includes the pros and cons of intershelving.

Jacobs, Peter J. "Nonprint Materials: A Low-Cost Treasure for Libraries." *Library Journal.* 114 (19) (November 1989): 58–59.
    Advocates equal treatment for all library materials in selection, acquisition, cataloging, shelving, and circulation.

Lewis, Shirley. "Nonprint Materials in the Small Library." *Library Resources & Technical Services.* 29 (2) (April/June 1985): 145–50.
    Includes a discussion of intershelving in a small library.

Lora, Pat. "Open Shelves for Video and Security for All." *Wilson Library Bulletin.* 65 (1) (September 1990): 74–75.
  The selection of a security system is discussed.
Mazikana, Peter C. "A Strategy for the Preservation of Audiovisual Materials." *Audiovisual Librarian.* 14 (1) (February 1988): 24–28.
  An exploration of the problems of acquisition and storage in third world countries.
Pittman, Randy. "AV Frontier." *Wilson Library Bulletin.* 63 (3) (November 1988): 90–91.
  A discussion about the ways of preventing videocassette theft and undesirable additions to tapes.
Spruit, Ed. *Audiovisual Media in the Dutch Public Library,* edited by the IFLA Round Table on Audiovisual Media. AV in Action, 2. The Hague: Nederlands Bibliotheek en Lektuur Centrum, 1983.
  This report of a five-year study applauds open access integrated storage and includes a description of suitable packaging. Illustrated with photographs.
Tiffany, Constance J. "The War Between the Stacks." *American Libraries.* 9 (8) (September 1978): 499.
  A brief, but forceful argument for intershelving.
Whiting, Ralph; Hagaman, Joseph; and Mallory, Dale. *Audiovisual Equipment Security.* Manitowoc, WI: Wisconsin Audiovisual Association, 1979.
  Well-illustrated, easy-to-understand instructions for marking and security equipment.
Whitney, Paul. "Libraries Increase Video Commitment." *Feliciter.* 34 (5) (May 1988): 9.
  This survey of ½ inch video collections in 35 Canadian libraries contains statistics on open access.
Wilkinson, David W. *Media Integration in Community College and Public Libraries.* [S.1.]: ERIC, 1986. (ED 284 543)
  Recommends total integration in shelving, catalog, and functional areas.

Part I
Introducing Intershelving into the Library

Chapter 1
The Care and
Handling of Staff

A community college hired a new chief librarian to administer a group of libraries in which the previous chief librarian had recently inaugurated intershelving. The new chief librarian was an enthusiastic supporter of the concept, noting that the circulation of all materials had risen and was continuing to rise. She received favorable comments from both academic staff and students concerning the rearranged shelving. However, little by little, almost imperceptively over the next two years, certain types of materials were withdrawn from the shelves and moved to the workroom or other enclosed areas to the point where the collection ceased to be integrated and had to be considered segregated. When asked, the staff gave a variety of reasons why, in their opinion, intershelving was unsatisfactory. A thorough investigation of the reasons for the failure of intershelving revealed that intershelving had been imposed upon the staff without consultation. The staff had resented the arbitrary imposition of inter-shelving, resulting in the conscious or unconscious determination to prove that this shelving method would not work. Despite the chief librarian's belief that intershelving was a superior system for the library, it was abandoned because of the staff's attitude.

Intershelving works wonderfully with a staff committed to the concept; it will work poorly when the staff is hostile or unenthusiastic. It is important that intershelving be introduced in ways that will gain the staff's coopera-tion. People tend to be apprehensive of change and many are afraid of appearing awkward and incompetent in using new types of materials and equipment. These fears generate negative attitudes and threaten the success of intershelving.

When nonbook materials are new to a library or have been stored in a separate area, many staff members will know little about them. Before intershelving is inaugurated, it is wise to spend time with the staff on the care and handling of different types of materials, e.g., how to remove a sound disc from a slipcase, how to rewind a filmstrip. This will have three benefits. First, it will make the staff feel more comfortable with the different materials. Second, proper handling will lengthen the life of all materials. Third, patrons are more likely to handle materials properly if staff members do so. It is important that staff members set the example.

In these times of economic restraint most staff members are very busy and have numerous responsibilities. Staff should be made aware that intershelving will release them from the necessity of fetching materials from other areas. Patrons will not ask where to find the nonbook items they want because all items on a subject will be in one area. The staff will have more time to devote to creative work.

An intershelved collection is a patron-oriented collection. Staff members who wish to provide good public service will appreciate intershelving when it is explained. One is led to believe from reading professional literature that all libraries, except those with an archival function, are devoted to the service of their particular publics. However, personal experience and conversations with other librarians and library users support the view that some libraries are operated in a manner most convenient for the staff. These staff members at best give lip service to the patron-oriented concept but resist implementation by voting with their feet. The ways of changing staff attitudes is a broader topic than the scope of this book includes. It is mentioned here by way of noting that management may first have to deal with staff attitudes to public service before intershelving can be discussed.

Each staff member who will be involved with the collection should be given at least one task during the preparation for intershelving. Such tasks could include written instructions on the operation of a piece of equipment or on proper handling techniques for a particular medium. These tasks are described more fully in the next chapter. This early involvement in intershelving can be continued after implementation by assigning to each appropriate staff member in turn an exhibit on a particular topic using all types of media. If only one staff member or a group of staff members is given these tasks, the rest of the staff tends to think that it is none of their affair.

There may be staff members who would be delighted to demonstrate avocational skills. Amateur carpenters can build special shelving; weekend artists can decorate low-cost containers. If staff members are too pressed for time to do these things, volunteers might be recruited. Senior citizens who would be bored shelving may be happy to donate their time when it involves skills in which they take pride. Staff or volunteers who contribute directly to a project become interested in making that project a success.

Time spent in preparing the staff for intershelving will be repaid in cooperation, increased public service, and time saved in the future.

Chapter 2
The Care and Handling of Patrons

People need help to become good library patrons. This is especially true when nonbook materials are introduced into the shelving system. As a first step the library should announce its new shelving policy in an interesting and informative manner. An attractive poster placed near the entrance may serve this purpose best. And well-labelled shelves are a necessity in a browsing collection.

Because many patrons will be unfamiliar with both materials and equipment, it is important to provide information about proper handling techniques. A study[1] of user satisfaction with, and ways for learning the operation of, an online public access catalog offers some insights that are pertinent to the provision of information about nonbook materials and equipment. The findings revealed a low level of user satisfaction with library staff instruction on a one-to-one basis. This is not surprising since staff members are likely to have limited time available for an individual patron and, in addition, possess varying levels of instructional skills. Despite the staff's efforts, the patron may not be able to remember these verbal instructions when the item is used. This method is not recommended because it consumes much time for a low return.

The study found that brochures and/or printed aids produced the most user satisfaction:

> The high level of satisfaction which resulted from learning by the use of brochures and printed aids suggests that this is an essential part of the user training program. Brochures and other printed aids provide a relatively low cost method of training large numbers of users. This approach is well suited for the independent learner.[2]

Instructions should be attached to the item in a prominent place where they are not likely to be overlooked but where they will not interfere with other necessary information, e.g., inside the lid of a container or on the blank verso of a manual's front cover. Instructions will thus be available when needed. There are two kinds of instructions: those relating to the operation of equipment and those relating to the care and handling of materials. Depending on the nature of the items borrowed, one or both types should be included in the package being circulated. For example, a map should have instructions about its care attached while a sound disc should have instructions about the operation of equipment as well as advice about the proper care and handling of the disc itself. Such instructions are written for a type of material or equipment, not for an individual item. To do the latter would be an overwhelming task.

This does not apply to equipment purchased for the use of patrons. In this case, instructions for the specific equipment must accompany each piece whether it is operated only in the library or is available for circulation.

In addition to these formal instructions, some of the bookmarks distributed by a library might advertise points about the care of various library materials.

In order to test the comprehensibility of the manufacturer's instructions received with most equipment, the instructions should be given to someone with little or no knowledge of the operation of library equipment. If s/he experiences any difficulty understanding how to operate the equipment, the instructions should be rewritten in a "step one, step two" fashion. In some instances, a diagram may be the best way to convey necessary information.

If a library has a severe staff shortage and cannot accommodate even the small amount of time it takes to include an instruction sheet when processing certain items, the next best way to bring this information to the attention of the patron is to have handouts arranged on or near the circulation desk backed by a big poster directing patrons to take one with the material they check out. Many patrons are intimidated by equipment. The sheet of instructions will help, but patrons may need friendly human contact to overcome the fear of looking awkward or incompetent. A word or two indicating that help is available if needed may give confidence.

Proper care and handling techniques can also be advertised on posters placed around the library. One way of bringing attention to these instructions is to place them on display systems that can be moved easily from time to time. Because of the novelty of its position, curiosity may induce patrons to read the display. Even more effective would be a display that can not only be moved easily but also dismantled and reassembled in a different configuration.[3]

Exhibits can be very effective as well. An analog sound disc left in the sun on the back seat of a car or a computer disk that has served as a resting place for a hot cup of coffee capture attention in an exhibit and are likely to make an impact that will be remembered.

Many libraries offer training sessions for patrons on different pieces of equipment, e.g., 16-mm motion picture projectors. Although the study discussed above reported that formal instruction had the second highest level of user satisfaction, it stated these limitations:

> The cost of this approach is high in terms of staff and would be extremely high if large numbers of users are to be taught. A formal instruction program does not appear to meet the needs of the independent learner. Formal instruction programs, even if closely scripted, are subject to inconsistent delivery. A further limitation of a formal instruction is that it is not necessarily available at times it is required by users.[4]

Aversions to machinery will be reinforced if equipment is in bad repair or if lighting in a room causes difficulty in reading a screen. Before deciding on the placement of equipment with screens, staff should operate them in different positions at various times of the day so that undesired reflections from light sources can be avoided.

A box of lintless cloths may be placed in the library for the use of patrons who are experiencing difficulties in the correct handling of media. Lintless cloths can be purchased or lintless sewing scraps can be donated by staff and patrons. The poster that directs attention to the box should list what types of cloths are lintless, so that people will be alerted to the proper donations and/or the correct cloths to use at home if an emergency arises, as well as pointing out when, why, and how lintless clothes may be used when handling media.

Furthermore, patrons should be encouraged by both staff and posters to use pencils rather than pens when taking notes. Pens may leak and may cause marks that are more difficult to remove than pencil marks. While some types of materials are not as sensitive to pressure as others, patrons should be actively discouraged from writing on paper placed on top of library materials.

Patrons may appreciate facilities for previewing some media, such as an illuminated light box for slides and filmstrips. Some libraries have lengths of transparent perspex with grooves designed to hold filmstrips rigid while held to a light or on a light box. These devices are not expensive and may minimize handling while the patron is making selection decisions. However, descriptive information on external labels may be equally effective and will limit unnecessary handling.

Assessing Damages

All materials deteriorate eventually. Handling of any sort contributes to this deterioration; rough handling speeds it. A library should establish criteria as to what constitutes normal wear and tear and apply these criteria consistently when assessing damage to materials. It is not reasonable to accept without penalty a book returned with a loose signature while charging for a scratched sound disc. Money will have to be spent repairing or replacing the book. A rebound book with its narrowed inner margin is less satisfying to use, as is the scratched disc. An inconsistent policy will discourage the use of materials for which there is a heavier damage penalty.

If a penalty is to be assessed, there needs to be an established method of indicating both existing damage before the item is loaned and any additional damage on return. Hostile reactions to damage charges may be minimized if the policy on punitive damage and the method of determining the charge is displayed prominently.

Patrons will report damage or loss if the consequences of doing so do not result in unreasonable fines. A statement encouraging the reporting of damage or loss should be added to instruction sheets, posters, exhibits, etc. Patron cooperation can save staff time. In addition, time can also be saved and frustration avoided if missing parts are noted on the container or in another prominent place. When the missing parts seriously affect the utility of an item, it should be withdrawn from circulation.

Most people do not want to be destructive. Ignorance and carelessness may be at the root of the problems. Indeed, many people display cooperation and constructive attitudes toward matters involving the betterment of community life. For example, the response in many communities to the recycling of garbage through the curbside pick-up of bottles, newspapers, etc., has been overwhelming, far in excess of the most optimistic expectations of realistic politicians. Library staffs should use this climate of public concern to educate patrons about the preservation of library collections. Public goodwill, properly directed, can turn people into good patrons.

Volunteers

The use of volunteers for certain tasks is suggested in various parts of this book. In general, people who volunteer become more aware of library materials and their appropriate care and use, and they may bring fresh and innovative ideas to the care, handling, or storage of nonbook materials. Volunteers also become a bridge to the community by sharing their knowledge with relatives, friends, and possibly strangers. The stronger the rapport established between library staff and volunteers and the more volunteers feel their contributions are valued, the more effective their bridges to the community will be.

References

1. Joan M. Cherry and Marshall Clinton, "A Profile of User Background and User Satisfaction with the University of Toronto OPAC and the Implications for User Training and User Interfaces" In *ASIS '89: Proceedings of the 52nd ASIS Annual Meeting, Washington, D.C. October 30-November 2, 1989*, edited by Jeffrey Katzer, Gregory Newby ... (Medford, N.J.: American Society for Information Science, 1989), pp. 121–128.

2. Cherry, p. 125.

3. Thorold J. Tronrud, "A Home Built Display Unit for Extension Service," *Museum Quarterly*, vol. 15, no. 3 [i.e. 4] (January 1987): 27–28. Reprinted in *Focus*, v. 13, no. 4 (Autumn 1988): 36.

4. Cherry, p. 125.

Further Reading

"User Resistance to Microforms." *One-Person Library*. 4 (2) (June 1987): 1–2.
Suggested ways of making microforms more acceptable to patrons.

Watkins, Jim. "Patron Perception and Use of Popular Nonprint Materials in Public Libraries." *Public Libraries*. 26 (3) (Fall 1987): 109–12.
One of the results of this survey of 64 public libraries demonstrates that "patrons who visit public libraries in order to use nonprint tend to use print materials as well during their visit."

Chapter 3
The Care and Handling of Nonbook Materials

The optimum conditions for the care, handling, and storage of materials preclude their use. Perfect storage is incompatible with the function of a circulating collection since materials must be handled during receiving, cataloging, processing, shelving, and circulation. The desire to preserve materials must be balanced against public convenience. The suggestions offered in this and following chapters are designed to cause the least damage to nonbook materials while permitting a library to meet its objectives.

Conservation measures introduced during the processing of materials for the shelves are a wise investment because they are generally much simpler and less expensive than those involved in damage repair. At the same time, the amount of effort devoted to preserving a particular item should be weighed against the replacement cost and the nature of the subject content. For example, little effort should be devoted to the preservation of some road maps because they cost little or nothing and may be superceded next year.

Libraries that are concerned about the deterioration of their collections may wish to undertake a condition survey. This survey can provide a picture of a collection's state and establish priorities for remedial action. For example, many faded items in a collection may indicate inappropriate light levels; the presence of mold, the need to control humidity; and insect damage, the need for effective pest control measures. A condition survey can be done at the same time as stock taking or by summer students employed for that purpose. People who do the survey do not need to be trained in damage detection if they are provided with appropriately devised forms to complete.

Building Design and Environmental Conditions

The building itself or the area within a building that houses a library can be a positive or negative force for the conservation of its contents. Attics and basements should be avoided because heavy rain and melting snow may cause leaks, and floods can be disastrous. Fluctuations in temperature and relative humidity are among the more detrimental factors. Temperature changes cause contractions and expansions which will hasten the deterioration of many materials. Items made from several component materials absorb and lose heat, expand and contract at different rates leading to structural breakdown. Direct sunlight, lighting fixtures, heating units such as radiators and vents, and uninsulated outer walls can cause temperature fluctuations in nearby items.

Materials also absorb and lose moisture at different rates. Low humidity causes brittleness and static electricity which attracts dust. High humidity promotes mold, mildew, fungi, and oxidation. In addition to materials damage, mold that comes off on the hand can be a health concern.

Libraries should be air conditioned and a constant temperature and relative humidity maintained. The decision to lower temperatures and/or shut down air conditioning systems overnight or on weekends should be examined carefully in light of daily climactic conditions. A reasonable compromise must be struck between patron/staff comfort, the need to preserve materials, and economic considerations when deciding what temperature and relative humidity (RH) to maintain. The temperature and relative humidity recommended by experts for the storage of library materials vary somewhat, but fall within a fairly narrow range. Ellison reports in his series of slide/tape presentations on the care of various media that Library of Congress researchers list 69°F [21°C],[1] plus or minus 1°F, and 49% RH, plus or minus 3%, as the proper environment for a multimedia library. The National Library of Canada recommends 19°–20°C [66°–68°F] and 40–45% RH, plus or minus 5%.[2] Basing its figures for storage and exhibition areas on comfort as well as preservation factors, the National Museums of Canada provides the following guidelines: optimum temperature, 21°C [69°F], plus or minus 1.5°C; minimum acceptable temperature range, 20°C to 23°C [68°–73°F]; optimum RH, 50%; year round RH range, 47% to 53%; minimum acceptable RH for winter, 40%; maximum acceptable RH for summer, 55%; fluctuations not to exceed 3% RH daily or 5% RH monthly.[3] Thompson, whose booklet has been edited by the IFLA

Round Table on Audiovisual Media, states that 18°C [64°F], plus or minus 3°C, and 50% RH, plus or minus 10%, is acceptable for all library materials.[4]

Lighting presents another problem. Readers need light. Bright, sunny libraries have a welcoming look, and libraries have worked long and hard to rid themselves of the "dark, dusty" reputation. But light, especially sunlight, is damaging to nearly all library materials and its effects are irreversible. Everyone knows what happens to papers left on a windowsill or to curtains covering a south window. Therefore, windows should be protected by blinds or curtains; alternatively, window panes can be especially treated to filter ultraviolet rays which cause the damage. In the construction of a new building consideration should be given to overhanging roofs or balconies that minimize the effect of bright sunlight. Ultraviolet rays from fluorescent lighting can be reduced, but not eliminated, by fitting the tubes with special covers or by purchasing special coated tubes. Incandescent lighting does not emit high levels of ultraviolet rays, but it produces more heat and uses more energy than fluorescent lighting. A choice of the lighting system to be used should be made after an examination of all design criteria.

A well-maintained air conditioning system with regularly cleaned filters can reduce air contaminants to insignificant levels. Window units do not provide the protection achieved by central air conditioning systems. If air conditioning is an impossible dream, humidifiers and/or dehumidifiers should be installed. It is important that temperature and relative humidity be measured and recorded to provide indication and warning when corrective action is required. Many inexpensive measuring instruments are not reliable; the best instruments include recording units.

Insect and rodent infestations can be very destructive to library materials. Even the insects that do not feast on library materials can be a problem because some patrons may unthinkingly squash an insect crawling on the surface of an item that they are using. Pests are a particular problem in hot climates or those with high humidity. Many libraries employ professional exterminators to fight these infestations. However, the chemical pesticides used by many exterminators may constitute a health hazard even if the building is closed during treatment, since harmful chemical residues and byproducts may remain in the building for a long period of time. Before resorting to the use of chemicals, steps should be taken to prevent the entry of insects and rodents and to make buildings inhospitable to pests.

Good building construction and repair are very positive factors in preventing infestations. Cracks in walls and floors and spaces around the entrance of pipes, conduits, etc., should be filled. A regularly cleaned building with good air circulation, adequately lighted in the manner described above, promotes pest control, since darkness and excessive moisture create favorable environments for many insect species. An RH of 50% will discourage multiplication because insects will not find enough moisture in the materials they eat to survive. Food should be permitted only in the staff room, and this room located well away from library collections. Circulation staff should be trained to watch for signs of insects on returned materials.

Additional precautions should be taken in areas where pest control is a major concern. Exterior lighting should be placed some distance from any entrance to a building to lessen the likelihood that night-flying insects will enter with patrons. Shrubbery should be planted no closer than 1½ feet from a building. Air screens at entrances are effective for insect control. Unfortunately for people comfort, the lower the temperature the less likely unwanted pests; in buildings where pest control is a consideration the temperature should be as low as patron and staff comfort permits.

There are other hazards to be avoided as well. Cleaning materials should not be housed near the collection. Paint, cleaning solvents, turpentine, and similar materials give off fumes which may have an adverse effect on some materials. Plants should not be placed where water spills will damage the collection.

Untreated wooden shelves can exude acids. Because information on the length of time various woods emit acids is unreliable, it is wise to coat all sides of wooden shelves with a primer plus two coats of a high-quality, solvent-based acrylic paint or with two or three coats of polyurethane varnish. Allow the shelves to dry for several weeks before shelving materials. If these measures are not possible, some protection is provided by lining shelves with archival quality 100% ragboard. The National Library of Canada's wooden shelves in its microform reading room are covered with Mylar D. Where metal shelving is used, a baked enamel finish with electrostatic powders is preferred.[5]

In areas that house media which can be affected adversely by static electricity, anti-static carpets should be installed or carpets avoided altogether.

Cleanliness

As dust comes to rest on the surface of materials and equipment, it may combine with the oils left from handling or lubrication to produce dirt, or it may be wound into a reel of film, sound tape, or videotape, producing surface scratches. These scratches are likely to cause progressive reduction in the quality of images or sound reproduction.

Libraries should attempt to have as clean an environment as is possible without discouraging the use of materials by unreasonable rules. For example, although it is desirable, few patrons will wash their hands before touching materials. However, patrons can be shown the proper way to handle materials that will be damaged by fingermarks and skin oils. In addition, smoking, eating, and drinking in the library should be prohibited. Particles from smoke settle on materials and the crumbs and drops from food and drink attract insects which feed on the chemicals in paper and other materials.

All media should be clean before being added to the collection. In particular, donations should be carefully inspected for mold or insect infestation.

Workroom Supplies and Procedures

A well-equipped workroom will facilitate the proper care and handling of nonbook materials. A supply of lintless gloves or cloths, distilled water, and acid-free containers should be included in the supplies maintained in the workroom. The gloves/cloths will be readily available when materials are handled; the distilled water can be used for the inexpensive routine maintenance of some materials; and the presence of acid-free containers which are necessary housing for some media will ensure that unsuitable containers are not used "in the meantime." All of these are inexpensive or possibly free if staff or volunteers cooperate in bringing lintless scraps from home and saving containers previously used for film materials. The workroom should also contain a high-powered flexible lamp to enable an appraisal of disc surfaces, filmstrip scratches, etc., if the library has a policy of damage assessment.

A workstation devoted to the processing of new materials or the repair of existing collections may be a worthwhile addition to the workroom. This will encourage an efficient routine because tools and supplies will be readily available in one area, a well-defined center for a workflow that need not be interrupted by other tasks.[6]

Equipment Maintenance

Clean equipment will help keep software clean; it is usually easier to clean hardware than software. When equipment is not in use, openings should be closed, where possible, and dust covers replaced. (Some librarians, however, do not cover equipment while the library is open because they believe covers discourage use.) Equipment manuals usually suggest suitable cleaning fluids and outline a program of regular maintenance which will extend the life of the equipment. Systematic hardware maintenance is more likely if equipment manuals can be retrieved easily and staff members are conditioned to return them to the proper file after use.

The need for more frequent equipment maintenance may occur when cheap software is purchased because cheap software may also be lower quality software. For example, an "economy" videotape may be more likely to leave residue on VCR heads than a top quality tape.

It is unwise to attempt the cleaning of sophisticated equipment without specially trained staff. The cost of professional cleaning should be balanced against the possibility of damage by unskilled staff and the consequent cost of repairs or replacement.

Preventing Damage and Loss

Rubber bands, paper clips, adhesive tapes, and even the temporary use of post-it notes should be avoided because they contain acids that can cause deterioration or stains which are almost impossible to remove. Even archival pressure-sensitive tape is not advisable for long-term storage, and there is no general agreement about adhesives. Experts recommend Japanese paper or starch paste. Use soft linen tapes rather than string to hold parts of items together when items stored in bundles are made of materials that may be cut by string.

Software should not be forced on or off hardware. If software cannot be fitted or removed with relative ease, the equipment should be serviced. It may be cheaper to replace old equipment in poor condition than to purchase new software because of the damage caused by faulty hardware.

It is important to note that temperature differences between hardware and software will affect playback and may cause damage to the software. Media and equipment should be allowed to return to room temperature naturally before play; neither heating nor cooling should be hastened.

A circulating library must expect some mishaps when materials leave the building. Most materials will be returned in good condition and it is not economically feasible or politically desirable to examine all nonbook items for damage after every loan. Books are not examined on return. The best a library can do is to provide protective circulation containers and instructions on proper care and handling procedures. The containers must be sturdy enough to survive the hazards of casual handling. Some libraries report that before purchasing a bulk order of video or audio containers, a staff member drops a representative sample on the floor to see whether the fastener springs open on impact.

External labels on packages can play an important role in lessening the likelihood of damage and loss. The information on the labels should be comprehensive enough for patrons to weed out items that are not useful for their purposes, thereby minimizing the number of times a package is opened unnecessarily.

The labels on media that will be inserted into equipment must be firmly affixed because loose labels can cause havoc first to the machine and subsequently to the software. Adequate labelling of the components of an item will help to decrease the loss of parts by indicating the item to which the component belongs together with a statement of the library's ownership. It may not be possible or practical to label every part in every set. A decision about the amount of labelling will revolve around its cost effectiveness and the importance of the components to the utilization of the whole.

Many-part items can be weighed out and in on scales that are able to detect a difference of as little as one gram. The cost of such an expensive scale can be justified only if the collection includes numerous items made of many expensive or difficult-to-replace components. A public library in the Metropolitan Toronto area solves the multiple-part problem by photographing its toy collection when an item is in the cataloging process. One photographic print is retained in the cataloging department as a type of shelf list record and one is placed in an album in the children's department where it is used not only to ascertain whether all parts are present, but also to allow patrons to select for reserve toys that are out on loan. A third print might also be attached to the container lid of a multipart item. This would be helpful in establishing that all parts are present before the borrower uses and/or returns the package.

A library with a book return box must expect that some nonbook materials will be placed in the box despite requests that returns be made to the circulation desk. Crushing and twisting may be the result of deposit in all return boxes, but return boxes outside the library have additional hazards because they do not protect their contents from damaging temperatures. Several libraries report that book return box damage to nonbook materials has been substantially reduced or eliminated by having an inside return box and by circulating materials in padded book mailer envelopes when patrons acknowledge that items are likely to be placed in the return box. Polly reports that her library circulates computer disks housed in compact diskette carrying cases which are inserted into vinyl hang-up bags together with associated documentation.

> We ask that software not be returned in the bookdrops, but we find much
> of it is, and that it suffers no damage.[7]

In developing a policy statement on examination procedures and punitive charges for damage and loss, the basic consideration is cost. The very expensive media, such as 16-mm motion pictures, should be examined for damage. On the other hand, it is not cost effective for staff to check each part of a many-piece set when the replacement value of the set is less than the salary cost involved. Media should also be examined in instances where unrepaired minor damage will lead to serious destruction, e.g., torn sprocket holes may cause a 16-mm motion picture projector to chew up many feet of film.

Good care and handling will lengthen the life of a collection. A circulating library must provide information and entertainment while maintaining materials in a useful state. This is a delicate balancing act. The suggestions in later chapters for ways of caring for and handling specific media are made with this thought in mind.

References

1. The conversion formula used here and elsewhere in this book: conversion from Fahrenheit (F) to Celsius (C) = subtract 32 from F temperature and divide the result by 1.8; conversion from C to F = multiply the C temperature by 1.8 and add 32 to the result. Fractions have been taken up or down to the nearest whole number.

John W. Ellison and others have produced a number of slide/tape packages on the storage and care of various media. Buffalo: School of Information and Library Studies,

State University of New York, 1978-9; distributed by National Audiovisual Center, Washington, DC.

2. Joyce M. Banks, *Guidelines for Preventative Conservation*. Rev. ed. (Ottawa, ON: Council on Federal Libraries, Committee on Conservation/Preservation of Library Materials, 1987), p. 10.

3. Banks, p. 39.

4. Anthony Hugh Thompson, *Storage, Handling and Preservation of Audiovisual Materials*. AV in Action, 3 (The Hague: Nederlands Bibliotheek en Lektuur Centrum, 1983), p. 8.

5. Conversation with Jan Michaels and Anna Lehn, National Library of Canada, July 24, 1990.

6. James LaRue, *A Simple Workstation for the Conservation of Library Materials*. Conservation Correspondence Series, no. 4 (Carbondale, IL: Illinois Cooperative Conservation Program, 1984). Also published as: "The Book as an Artifact," *Illinois Libraries*, vol. 67, no. 8 (October 1985): 685–95.

These instructions for the design and equipment of a simple workstation include lists of tools, materials, and supplies, description of adhesives, cleaners, paper, film, etc.

7. Jean Polly, "Circulating Software: Some Sensible Groundrules," *Wilson Library Bulletin*, vol. 60, no. 10 (June 1986): 22.

Further Reading

Agaja, James Abayomi. "Effects of a Harsh Climate on Audiovisual Services in Libraries in Arid Regions: The Case of the Media Unit of Maiduguri University Library." *Audiovisual Librarian*. 14 (3) (August 1988): 126–28.
   A description of the effect of extreme daily temperature fluctuations and arid conditions.

Baish, Mary Alice. "Special Problems of Preservation in the Tropics." *Conservation Administration News*. 31 (October 1987): 4–5.

Barton, John P., and Wellheiser, Johanna G., eds. *An Ounce of Prevention: A Handbook on Disaster Contingency Planning for Archives, Libraries and Record Centres*. Toronto: Toronto Area Archivists Group Education Foundation, 1985.
   The rehabilitation of paper, photographic materials, magnetic tape, sound recordings, art works, and realia is included in this book.

Boomgaarden, Wesley L. "Preservation Planning for the Small Special Library." *Special Libraries*. 76 (3) (Summer 1985): 204–11.
   The causes of deterioration, preservation decision-making, and treatment operations to maximize the useful life of a collection are discussed.

Brezner, Jerome, and Luner, Philip. "Nuke 'Em! Library Pest Control Using a Microwave." *Library Journal*. 114 (5) (September 15, 1989): 60–63.
   Suggestions for a pest control program, a review of pest control methods, and a description of the positive result of the use of a microwave oven.

Davis, Mary. "Preservation Using Pesticides: Some Words of Caution." *Wilson Library Bulletin*. 59 (6) (February 1985): 386–88, 431.
   A discussion of the problems involved in pesticide use with some suggestions for alternate ways of controlling pests.

DeCandido, Robert. "Out of the Question." *Conservation Administration News.* 24 (January 1986): 15.
    A description of the effect of regular and archival pressure-sensitive tape on library materials.

Dureau, J.M., and Clements, D.W.G. *Principles for the Preservation and Conservation of Library Materials.* IFLA Professional Reports, no. 8. The Hague: IFLA Headquarters, 1986.

Harrison, Helen P. "Conservation and Audiovisual Materials." *Audiovisual Librarian.* 13 (3) (August 1987): 154–62.
    An overview of the archival preservation of various formats.

Johnson, Arthur W. *The Practical Guide to Book Repair and Conservation.* London: Thames and Hudson, 1988.
    Some of this well-illustrated book is pertinent to nonbook materials: the equipment and materials needed for repairs, insects and their control, environment, adhesives, and a list of U.K., U.S., and German suppliers.

Kyle, Hedi. *Library Materials Preservation Manual: Practical Methods for Preserving Books, Pamphlets and Other Printed Materials.* Bronxville, NY: N.T. Smith, 1983.
    Well illustrated with step-by-step instructions, this book includes information on the proper set-up of work areas, adhesives, folding, edge cutting, knots, the construction of pamphlet binders, and the cleaning and repair of paper.

Monitoring Temperature and Relative Humidity: Creating a Climate for Preservation. Andover, MA: Northeast Document Conservation Center, 1989. Typescript. Available free from University Products, Holyoke, MA.
    This nontechnical discussion of climate control includes descriptions of various monitoring devices.

Muñoz-Solá, Haydée. "Preservation of Library Materials in a Tropical Climate: The Puerto Rican Experience." *Science & Technology Libraries.* 7 (3) (Spring 1987): 41–47. Also published in *Preservation and Conservation of Sci-Tech Materials,* ed. by Ellis Mount. New York: Haworth Press, 1987.

Neitzke, Curt. "Getting the Most from Your AV Dollar." *Technicalities.* 5 (9) (September 1985): 11–15.
    Practical general guidelines for the selection of 16-mm projectors, videocassette recorders/players, 35-mm slide projectors/viewers, overhead and opaque projectors.

Neitzke, Curt. "The Library Tinker's Tool Kit." *Technicalities.* 4 (10) (October 1984): 14–15.
    A practical list of tools for the simple maintenance of audiovisual equipment and computer hardware.

Ogden, Sherelyn. "Treatment of Wooden Shelving for Books." *Conservation Administration News.* 27 (October 1986): 6.
    The information in this article is also pertinent to nonbook materials.

Parker, Thomas A. *Study of Integrated Pest Management for Libraries and Archives.* Paris: UNESCO, 1988.
    A description of various pests, the damage they cause, and their management.

Pasco, M.W. *Impact of Environmental Pollution on the Preservation of Archives and Records: A RAMP Study.* Paris: UNESCO, 1988.
    A point-form description of the nature of many pollutants and suggested anti-pollution strategies.

Raynes, Patricia. "Insects and Their Control in the Library." *Conservation Administration News.* 27 (October 1986): 4, 24–25.

Sanders, H. Michael. "Establishing a Preventive Maintenance Program for Media Equipment." *Ohio Media Spectrum.* 41 (3) (Fall 1989): 54–57.
Describes procedures for keeping equipment in sound, usable condition.

Schroeder, Don, and Lare, Gary. *Audiovisual Equipment and Materials: A Basic Repair and Maintenance Manual.* 2 vols. Metuchen, NJ: Scarecrow Press, 1979-1989.
Vol. 1 deals with techniques for the basic emergency repair of 16-mm sound film, filmstrips, and cassette tapes and the cleaning of analog sound discs; vol. 2 with videocassettes, CDs, videodiscs, and microcomputer software. Both volumes have clear instructions accompanied by illustrations.

Teo, Elizabeth A. "Conservation of Library Materials and the Environment: A Study with Recommendations." *Illinois Libraries.* 67 (8) (October 1985): 711–17.

Weinstein, Frances Ruth. "A Psocid by Any Other Name . . . (is Still a Pest)." *Library & Archival Security.* 6 (1) (Spring 1984): 57–66.
A description of book-lice, bookworms, cockroaches, silverfish, and termites; the damage they do; methods of extermination; and preventive control.

Winkle, Becky. "Preservation on a Shoestring: Low- and No-Budget Options to Get a Preservation Program Off the Ground." *American Libraries.* 16 (11) (December 1985): 778–79.
Suggestions for implementing a preservation program with no funding, $1000, and $3000 budgets. Includes a workstation description.

Advice on conservation and preservation is available from the following:

In Canada

Preservation Office
National Library of Canada
395 Wellington Street
Ottawa, Ontario
K1A 0N4

Moving Image, Data and Audio
  Conservation Division and
  Magnetic Media Division
National Archives of Canada
Ottawa, Ontario
K1A 0N3

Canadian Conservation Institute
1030 Innes Road
Ottawa, Ontario
K1A 0C8

In the United States

National Preservation Program
  Office
Library of Congress
101 Independence Avenue, S.E.
Washington, DC 20540

Conservation Services Referral
  System
Foundation of the American
  Institute for Conservation of
  Historic and Artistic Works
1400 16th Street, N.W.
Washington, DC 20036

Chapter 4
General Storage
Considerations

Total intershelving is the ideal arrangement for a browsing collection and should be effected wherever possible. This means that every item in the collection is housed in one classification sequence (see Figure 1). However, there may be reasons why this cannot be accomplished. For example, shelving space may be too limited to provide the 12½-inch-high space necessary for housing analog sound discs; an area may be subject to vibrations which affect videotapes; theft of sound cassettes may be a

Figure 1. Total intershelving.

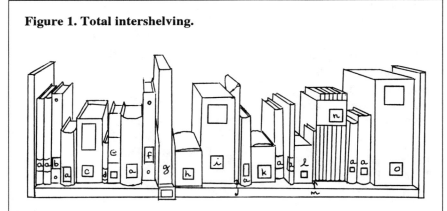

a. book; b. binder containing microfiches; c. box containing filmstrips; d. book-like album containing a single sound cassette; e. videocassette in container; f. binder containing slides; g. clip-on holder containing a motion picture in a box; h. motion picture loop cartridge in container; i. box containing slide carousel; j. envelope containing a single Viewmaster slide; k. microfilm reel in container; l. box containing microopaque cards; m. pamphlet binder containing a single picture; n. Princeton file holding issues of a current periodical; o. kit housed in a box problem. A good solution to such problems is to have well-labelled dummies act as surrogates in these areas. This allows some browsing and maintains the sequence. It is especially helpful if the labelling on surrogates includes clear instructions concerning where the item can be obtained.

Partial intershelving is a second solution in which all items are on open access, but they are not in one sequence. There are three types of partial intershelving:

1. Media in the same classification range are stored on one shelf. The items in boxes and other book-like containers are intershelved with books on one part of the shelf. Other media are housed in some type of storage device on another part of the shelf. This is the best method of partial intershelving because items with similar subject content are in close proximity.

2. Some media, housed in boxes and other suitable containers, are intershelved. Other media are stored on separate shelves, generally called media shelves, at the end of the appropriate classification sequence. This is satisfactory only in sections of the collection where the beginning of the classification sequence on the regular shelves is not widely separated from the beginning of the same sequence on the media shelves. Materials are likely to be overlooked if many shelves separate the two.

3. Far less satisfactory are freestanding storage units because these separate materials in a substantial way. These units are justified only when shelf space is limited and open floor storage is the only room left for collection expansion.

One or all of these methods of partial intershelving can be used in a library for a variety of reasons. One method may be applied to a particular type of material, another method to a particular storage area. All partial intershelving devices should be as flexible as possible to allow for the expansion of the collection. Dummies can also be used in partial intershelving where it is not possible to shelve a specific item in its proper sequence.

Devices for Intershelving

Some shelving is manufactured in differently shaped modules that can be assembled and disassembled easily to accommodate an expanding multimedia collection. These modules can be used for a total shelving system or only in sections of the classification where the flexibility afforded by modules is needed. Figure 2 demonstrates a possible arrangement of shelving modules.

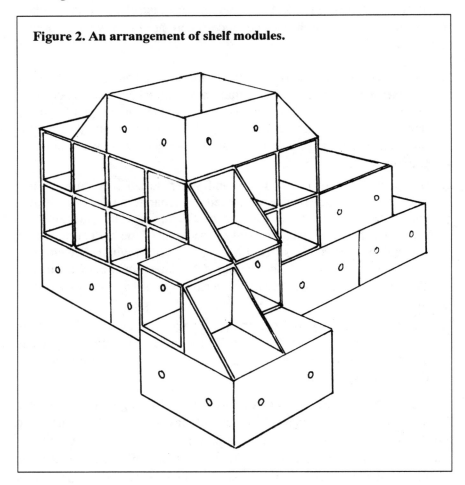

Figure 2. An arrangement of shelf modules.

Boxes and Pamphlet Boxes. Some manufacturers market their products in sturdy boxes that are designed for shelving and are adequately labelled. After processing, these boxes can be intershelved.

Unfortunately, some materials are packaged in containers that are not likely to endure reasonable handling, while some have no containers at all. The library worker is then faced with decisions.

If an item is in an attractive but inadequate box which is descriptive of its contents, an effort should be made to prepare it for shelving. Some manufacturers, in order to pare costs, do not reinforce corners. Reinforced corners may be all a box needs to make it durable. Boxes can also be strengthened with a covering of adhesive transparent sheeting. This may be expensive, but it might be worth the cost to preserve a truly useful box.

Some manufacturers package materials in boxes that are larger than needed for the contents and which, if shelved, would take up unnecessary space. These materials should be repackaged.

Boxes provide an easy, though not the only, means of intershelving. They sit on shelves very much like books and provide protection for their contents. There are many different types of boxes available both commercially and casually; the decision of what type of boxes to use for a particular medium depends on the nature of the material, the degree of preservation required, and the library's goals and objectives.

Materials that react to the chemicals in ordinary paper products, such as film, must be housed in acid-free boxes. An archival pen will provide a quick reading on acidity levels if there is some doubt whether a container is acid free. Items that are difficult to replace and will have a long-term use should be stored in boxes of archival quality. There are many types of archival boxes available commercially, but they are expensive.

There are also many types of nonarchival boxes for sale—cardboard, fiberboard, corrugated, plasticized, etc. Some have inserts that hold the contents in place. These can be found in any library supply company's catalog. Some of these boxes can be purchased flat at a lower cost and hand assembled in the library.

Opaque boxes interpose a barrier between an item and a patron, and this barrier is necessary for materials that are affected adversely by light. Other materials are made more accessible by housing them in transparent plastic boxes, pamphlet boxes, or Princeton files. However, Princeton files are useful only for items that are large enough to be held securely in the file. Pamphlet boxes are available in many colors and several styles, e.g., cut corner, open back, cardboard, plastic, corrugated, with and without finger-holes for easy removal from the shelves. The cheapest ones are purchased flat and assembled by the library staff.

It is easy for library staff to obtain commercially made boxes; most library supply companies display a variety of boxes in their catalogs. Therefore, the following discussion will concentrate on economical boxes not marketed in these catalogs.

Inexpensive box cutouts can be purchased flat from a local box manufacturer and assembled easily by library staff. This very low-cost packaging can be even cheaper if ordered by a group of libraries because a larger run will result in lower unit costs.

If library staff have slack periods or volunteer help is available, boxes and other enclosures can be made. Many easy-to-follow instructions have been published; some of these are cited in the list of Further Reading at the end of this chapter and in the General Bibliography. Library-made enclosures may be especially useful for oversize or unusually shaped materials.

Some boxes may be acquired casually—library supply boxes, gift boxes, etc. Staff members can be alerted to preserve sturdy boxes for use in storage. Local druggists or camera stores may be willing to donate used boxes, many of which will be acid free.

Unfortunately, the great majority of low-cost boxes are unattractive and some casually acquired boxes, such as shoe boxes, may have unwanted information written on them. This information can be covered with leftover paint or wallpaper. An attractive brochure should be kept until the item is received and then used to decorate a noninformative container.

It takes time to make cheap boxes attractive, but this may have benefits for the library. In addition to obtaining attractive boxes, a school library can advertise its nonbook collection by cooperating with an art teacher and a public library can gain publicity by holding a contest for the creation of appropriate box decoration. The activity associated with box decoration also offers an opportunity to reach out to a new group of people. There are individuals who would not volunteer to shelve but would be happy to use their artistic talents. For instance, someone who enjoys wrapping presents may find decorating media boxes a challenge.

Even if staff members or volunteers are not available for box decoration, a brief description of the contents and equipment needed for utilization should be prominently displayed on the front of the box to increase the ease of browsing and reduce the amount of handling. In a library with a card catalog, an extra catalog card could be used for this purpose; in an automated system, a printout of a catalog record stripped of its MARC coding. A catalog card or catalog record that includes a summary is particularly useful.

Book-like Albums. These containers have been designed in response to an expressed interest in intershelving and are available in a wide range of sizes adapted for particular media or various combinations of media. The albums generally have vinyl covers and rigid plastic interiors molded to hold specific numbers and types of media. The "snap-in" compartments maintain a firm hold on sound cassettes, videocassettes, compact disc jewel boxes/cases, filmstrip canisters, and slide carousels. Some have permanently affixed boxes in which slides can be stored. Many have clear plastic pockets for manuals, charts, and other two-dimensional materials. In some albums a spine window allows a patron to read the title on a filmstrip canister lid or on a cassette container.

There are three features that detract from these otherwise useful albums. The first is price. They are more expensive than many other storage methods described in this book. Second, they are less flexible. They are designed for a specific medium or combination of media; other storage methods, e.g., boxes, binders, hang-ups, can be used by a variety of media. For example, if a filmstrip housed in a hanging bag is discarded, the bag can be used to store another medium. Third, many albums are designed to house slide carousels, sound and/or videocassettes without their protective containers. The less expensive albums do not have closures that protect contents from dust and dirt, which can affect the quality of tape playback and damage slides. These media should be housed in the more expensive albums that lock with a dust-tight closure (see Figure 3).

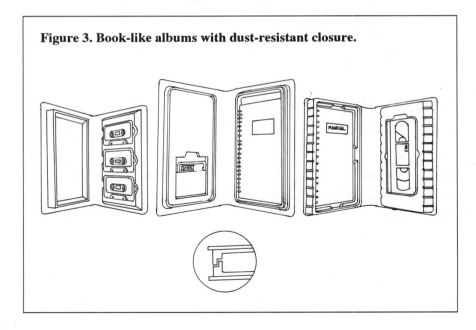

Figure 3. Book-like albums with dust-resistant closure.

There are some book-like albums made of paper products designed to hold one or two cassettes and cartridges. These storage units may be preferred for some media because they accommodate containers and are cheaper to purchase.

Binders. Intershelving can be accomplished very effectively by housing media in suitable binders made of materials rigid enough to be self-supporting. Cloth-bound binders are preferable to those covered with plastic because polyvinyl chloride (PVC) is used in the manufacture of many binders with plastic covers. PVC is unstable, and the gases emitted will damage some types of media.

Ring binders are particularly versatile because plastic pages (made of a stable plastic) designed to hold various sizes and shapes can be purchased or library-made. These transparent pages allow the items to be browsed easily yet keep them protected from direct contact with fingers. The whole binder can be circulated or individual pages can be removed for circulation. Ring binders receive rough handling from students in their school work and most will certainly stand up to the gentler demands of normal library use. Avoid loading a binder to the point that its contents are under pressure. If many pages must be stored, those housed in a binder with D rings are less likely to be distorted than those stored in one with O rings.

A library may wish to shelve a single item but may not want to use the space or be able to afford the cost of a ring binder. In this case the item can be housed in a pressboard pamphlet binder by attaching:

1.   One-sheet items to any convenient place inside the binder;
2.   Items with a single fold to the spine of the binder;
3.   Items with more than one fold to an inside edge.

A set that is too large for a ring binder can be placed in an open back pamphlet tie binder or a hinge binder. There are several fasteners that can be used to secure a binder's contents, all with some disadvantages. Tie and button fasteners protrude and may be torn or loosened in reshelving; velcro grabs dust, fibers from clothing, etc.; magnetic closures cannot be used for media that will be affected by magnets or stored or handled near such media.

Envelopes. Envelopes suitable for storage purposes are available commercially in various sizes; many types can be made easily by library staff or volunteers. They should be composed of nonacidic materials and have closing flaps that will protect their contents from dust and dirt, constructed so that the opening and closing of a flap will not damage the enclosed materials.

Envelopes can be used as storage containers in one of two ways: the envelopes themselves may be intershelved or envelopes may be placed in a larger container (a) for the added protection of the whole item; (b) as a method of preserving the fragile parts of an item; (c) as a way of gathering discrete items or sets in a subject group housed in one container.

Envelopes intershelved by themselves need to be rigid enough to support their contents. In some cases, it may be necessary to insert archival quality bristol board to give this support.

The decision to use paper or plastic envelopes will depend on the type of materials to be contained and a library's policies about circulation and storage.

Paper envelopes are opaque and porous, protecting their contents from the adverse effects of light and accumulation of moisture. They are easier to write on than plastic and, in general, less expensive to purchase. Paper envelopes can be obtained in bright colors which add visibility to an intershelved item. Because seams can be a problem for some materials, they should be situated at the sides and/or the bottom of an envelope, and nonacidic adhesive used in an envelope's manufacture. Paper envelopes buffered to an alkaline pH are best for the long-term storage of paper materials, nonbuffered neutral pH high alpha cellulose envelopes for the long-term storage of film materials. The biggest disadvantage of paper envelopes is that the contents must be removed during browsing and use, promoting deterioration from abrasion, fingermarks, etc.

Conversely, plastic envelopes allow viewing, and in some instances the use of, materials without removal from the envelope, and the seams present less problem because they have been formed by heat sealing. If plastic envelopes are closed too tightly, moisture can be trapped. Polyester, polypropylene, triacetate, and polyethylene are chemically stable and have a neutral pH; these materials are listed above in the general order of their rigidity from most to least rigid, although there is some variation in different types of envelopes made from a particular kind of plastic. In addition to supplying less support, the less rigid are the most easily scratched. The most rigid and inert, polyester, generates the most static electricity which attracts dust and is the most expensive. Although inexpensive and abrasive-resistant, polyvinyl chloride (PVC) envelopes should not be used because they are not chemically stable and will cause deterioration of their contents over time.

Clip-on Holders. Clip-on holders are excellent units for intershelving for those librarians who want to shelve their collections with as little repackaging as possible. Unfortunately, I searched in vain for these very useful holders in recent catalogs of the library supply companies represented at American, Canadian, and Ontario library association conventions. The holders were designed for either wood or steel shelves. Both styles were surprisingly inexpensive; those designed for steel shelves were two-thirds the cost of those for wood shelves. Prices were competitive with corrugated fiberboard containers and cheaper than corrugated plastic containers and vinyl book-like containers. Perhaps some small manufacturers are producing them, or can be persuaded to do so. With this hope in mind, and with the assumption that these holders are still in use, I will describe and discuss them here.

Clip-on holders exist in several sizes suitable for a variety of materials. Because they are self-supporting, they can be placed anywhere on the shelves.

The holders are attached to the shelves by built-in bracket clips. When holders house one item, one set, or items with the same classification number, the call number or classification can be affixed to the clip on the lower front edge of the shelf. This aids quick shelving and the identification of items with spines too narrow to permit their labels to be seen immediately.

Almost-shelf-tall, narrow units give support to items that cannot stand vertically by themselves such as pictures, maps, transparencies, sound discs, videodiscs, and microcomputer disks. Filmstrips are held firmly in slanted clip-ons, which may have a compartment for manuals. Small items, such as sound tapes, and microfilms, which could be pushed inadvertently out of sight to the back of the shelf, are kept in their proper places by shallow clip-ons. There are clip-ons designed for small multimedia kits. Their steel construction is not only self-supporting but also supports adjacent materials, and some libraries use these units as bookends. In this position the holders become devices for partial intershelving. The same steel construction also makes them almost impervious to destruction from normal library handling. However, they cannot accommodate the range of media or number of items possible with other types of devices.

Modular Units. A modular unit is another device that will hold small items at the front of the shelf. Cube or similarly shaped units specially designed to hold sound and microcomputer cassettes or 16-mm microfilm reels or 35-mm microfilm reels can be shelved singly or can be attached together, both horizontally and vertically, to house a many-piece set. They are sturdy enough to withstand normal library use and are reasonably priced. One side of the unit is open so that labels can be seen. The units are spacious enough to accommodate a container, which gives added protection to the item being stored.

Other units, sometimes called "mini-cabinets," have similar characteristics but do not lock together. Each unit holds more than twice the number of items and is approximately the same per unit cost as interlocking modules. Double size "mini-cabinets" are available; however, capacity can be increased by placing single units side by side.

Devices designed for book, periodical, and pamphlet storage can also be used to house nonbook materials. Examples of such devices are the "DecoRack" or the "File Frame," both plastic units with adjustable dividers and one open side, and the "Add-A-File," marketed as a desk-top vertical file system that can accommodate any number of materials by adding interlocking units.

Interlocking units are better suited to intershelving because they are more flexible. Both types of modules can be used for partial intershelving by placing a single unit or several units on one end of a shelf.

Devices for Partial Intershelving

Hanging Devices. The most popular hanging storage devices appear to be hanging bags because they are inexpensive and versatile. The bags are available in ten sizes to accommodate items with a variety of shapes. Their clear polyethylene construction allows the patron to see the contents, thereby reducing the handling of individual items.

There are three storage methods for hanging bags:

1. Part shelf storage. Free standing racks, which are available in several sizes, are placed at one end of a shelf in the appropriate classification sequence. This method of hanging bag storage is preferred because it keeps the contents of the bags closer to similarly classified materials than the other two methods.

When there is only one bag to be housed on a particular shelf, libraries that have wire bookends suspended from the underside of the shelf above can use these as the hanging device.

2. Separate shelf for hanging bag device. This is a variation of the media shelf discussed later in this chapter, in which a whole shelf is devoted to the storage of nonbook materials. It is situated at the end of the shelves holding books and, possibly, book-like containers with the same classification. This method has three advantages over media shelves; it can hold a larger range of sizes; manuals can be stored with the items; and intershelving items within the device is not hampered by partitions.

    If a library has closed end shelving, the bags can be hung on an adjustable tension rod held by free standing supports. If a library has open end shelving, the bags can be hung on a rod supported at each end by brackets attached to the standards for the rest of the shelving.

3. Storage outside the shelves. A library that has limited shelf space may store hanging bags outside the regular shelving. A bar can be mounted on a section of the wall not used for shelving or even on a suitable door. If the available wall space is very small, the bags can be hung on utility brackets attached to the wall near the appropriate classification. This is an excellent way of using odd bits of space in cramped quarters. Bags can also be hung from pegboard brackets. Pegboard can be cut to fit any space.

    Revolving floor stands for storing bags can be used if no wall space is available. These should be placed as close to the appropriate classification as possible. These stands are much more expensive and less effective than the other storage devices for hanging bags.

There are other more sophisticated hanging device systems designed to house specific formats such as maps, technical drawings, or sound discs. Some of these can be adapted to partial intershelving. They are much more expensive than hanging bags.

Large items can be hung on dress racks or other types of hanging devices not normally found in libraries. Sometimes these racks can be purchased cheaply at distress sales.

Racks. Racks placed at the end of a classification sequence are another useful method for the partial intershelving of many media. Racks can be purchased in a variety of sizes and shapes. Wire racks and sorter racks have fixed dividers, while racks that are frequently called "book trays" have adjustable dividers/supports.

It is important that racks are not filled to the point where materials are damaged by pressure from dividers. Dividers should be high enough to support materials that may be tilted when items near them are removed. For example, a divider that supports only the lower half of a sound disc may increase the likelihood of warpage.

Cheap wire racks that may rust and racks coated with polyvinyl chloride, an unstable compound which breaks down emitting harmful gases, should be avoided.

Media Shelf. Some libraries prefer to house nonbook materials on a separate shelf. For example, there may be several shelves of books in the Dewey decimal classification sequence 520–529, followed by a shelf of small- to medium-sized nonbook materials and a shelf of large items, each arranged in the 520–529 sequence. A shelf without special fittings to assist the housing of nonbook materials is not termed a "media shelf." Indeed, large items are frequently placed on a bottom or top shelf. A media shelf is designed specifically to house nonbook materials and is usually tilted at a 45° angle to facilitate browsing.

Many commercially produced media shelves have devices that hold specific types of media in rigid or semi-rigid positions. One of the most flexible and inexpensive is pictured in Figure 4. This shelf is fitted with bars that can be adjusted when the collection is shifted. This type of shelf is preferred to a shelf with fixed slots because it easily accommodates newly cataloged items in their proper place in the classification. If a new item is to be housed in a media shelf with rigid partitions, all other items with classification numbers following the one on the new item will have to be moved individually, a time-consuming task.

Unfortunately, commercial media shelves do not accommodate manuals.

Cartmobiles. Cartmobiles are book trucks adapted for media storage. They are generally used to solve two problems. First, if a library's shelf space cannot accommodate an increase in the collection, book trucks with fittings to house nonbook materials can increase storage space. Second, materials too large to fit easily on regular shelves can be housed on book trucks with flat shelves.

In both cases the book truck should be positioned as close as possible to the shelves containing materials with the same subject content.

Figure 4. Separate media shelf.

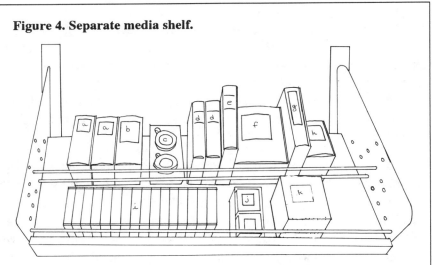

a. motion picture loop cartridge in container; b. microfilm reel in container; c. filmstrip canister in holder; d. sound tape reel in container; e. CD set in container; f. 8-mm motion picture reel in container; g. small game in box; h. flash cards in box; i. sound cassette in container; j. slides in semi-transparent box; k. realia in container

Limited-Space Storage. Staff in libraries with limited space face a constant challenge in making their collections browsable. Some methods for coping with this problem have been described above under "Hanging Devices" and "Cartmobiles." There are many types of wall-mounted devices available commercially, such as those named "hot files," "data racks," "literature racks," "newspaper displayers," "hook and rail systems," which can house various materials. These may be mounted on walls near appropriate shelves, on little-used doors, on the end of solid-end stacks, or on other available spaces.

Devices with hangers can be suspended from the ends of open-end shelves or from bars attached to walls.

Velcro offers another way to use limited space. Velcro stands may be purchased or boards covered with velcro fastened to walls. Velcro patches can be used in a variety of ways to attach holding devices or storage containers.

In all cases, attempts should be made to place materials housed outside shelves as close to their correct place in the classification sequence as possible.

Further Reading

Anthony, L.J., ed. *Handbook of Special Librarianship and Information Work.* 5th ed. London: Aslib, 1982.
  One chapter gives an overview of storage and intershelving for transparencies, slides, filmstrips, filmloops, motion pictures, analog sound discs and tapes, and videotapes.

Brown, Margaret R., with the assistance of Etherington, Don, and Ogden, Linda K. *Boxes for the Protection of Rare Books: Their Design and Construction.* A National Preservation Program Publication. Washington, DC: Library of Congress, 1982.
  Well-illustrated step-by-step instructions for archival boxes which can be applied to containers for nonbook materials.

Fothergill, Richard, and Butchart, Ian. *Non-book Materials in Libraries: A Practical Guide.* 2nd ed. London: Bingley, 1984. (3rd ed. announced for publication 1990)
  Pages 236–49 have an overview of the intershelving of portfolios containing paper or photographic prints, slides, filmstrips, microforms, motion pictures, computer disks, analog sound discs and tapes, transparencies, and videotapes, with particular emphasis on labelling.

Korty, Margaret Barton. *Audio-visual Materials in the Church Library: How to Select, Catalog, Process, Store, Circulate, and Promote.* Riverdale, MD: Church Library Council, 1977.
  Suggestions for the intershelving and/or partial intershelving of filmstrips, slides, motion pictures, transparencies, stereographs, sound recordings, pictures, and maps; and for mounting and reinforcement of pictures and maps.

Langrehr, John S., and Russell, Anne. "Audiovisual Packaging and Shelving." *Audiovisual Instruction.* 22 (9) (November 1977): 12–14.
  A detailed description of a packaging system suitable for intershelving developed by an Australian library.

Library of Congress. National Preservation Office. *Fact Sheet: Plastics Used in Preservation.* Preservation Information Series: Materials and Standards. Washington, DC: Library of Congress, 1987. Typescript. Free.
  A description of various plastics used for the conservation of library materials.

Morrow, Carolyn Clark, and Dyal, Carole. *Conservation Treatment Procedures: A Manual of Step-By-Step Procedures for the Maintenance and Repair of Library Materials.* 2nd ed. Littleton, CO: Libraries Unlimited, 1986.
  Well-illustrated, easy-to-follow instructions, which include a list of equipment and supplies and approximate time and cost per item for pamphlet binding; mending with Japanese paper, starch paste, and heat set tissue; polyester film encapsulation; simple portfolios; phase boxes and double tray boxes.

Schlefer, Elaine R. "Wrappers with Magnetic Closures." *Abbey Newsletter.* 10 (5) (October 1986): 74–76.

Part II
Storage of Various Media for Greater Access

Chapter 5
Analog Sound Discs

"The end is near for vinyl record" states the headline for a newspaper article. A customer hoping to purchase an analog sound disc now walks past bins of analog sound tapes and digital sound discs, commonly called compact discs or CDs, to a small collection of analog vinyl discs at the back of a music store. Sales of vinyl albums now account for less than 4 percent of recording industry sales in the United States. Most record companies have stopped issuing classical and country music recordings on vinyl discs and are reducing the number of popular music discs available in this format. The newspaper article forecasts that in a few years vinyl discs will become a specialty business by small companies.[1]

There is a medium- or long-term end in sight for vinyl discs in most circulating collections. These discs are fragile and may not be easily replaced when damaged. As fewer vinyl sound discs are produced, patrons may move to CD or digital audiotape (DAT) systems, and the circulation of vinyl discs will decline. However, as the demand for this service will continue in the immediate future, so will the need for suggestions about the care, handling, and storage of vinyl discs.

The focus of this chapter is on the 12-inch, $33^1/_3$ rpm-long-playing, analog, vinyl sound disc format. Much of the content can also be applied to the 7-inch diameter, 45-rpm, analog, vinyl sound discs found in some collections.

The size and fragility of analog sound discs discourages many libraries from incorporating them into their intershelved collections. Some libraries do not have sufficient shelf space to allow 12½-inch-high shelves in sections where only a few discs would be stored. In these instances, open access storage close to the appropriate classification section may be advisable. The same approach may be taken when libraries possess only music sound discs, all of which would be shelved in a small range of classification numbers.

Different methods of storage, ranging from total intershelving to "nonshelf" open access devices, may be used in various sections of the collection depending on the numbers of discs to be housed. For example, libraries that have spoken-word as well as music discs may intershelve the former, while placing the latter in "nonshelf" open access devices.

Another factor to be taken into consideration when making storage decisions is the heavy weight of analog sound discs. If a library does not have heavy-duty shelving, it must limit the number of discs to be placed on any one shelf or, possibly, section of shelving.

Care and Handling

Warping. If a disc slipcase is received in a cellophane wrapper, the wrapper should be removed immediately. It is highly sensitive to temperature change and may shrink, causing the disc to warp. Warping can also be caused by housing discs near sources of heat or by improper storage methods.

Several people with home disc collections suggested methods for restoring warped discs to their original shape. All of these follow the same procedures, only the source of heat differs—a heat lamp, natural sunlight, a pilot light. I could not verify any of these methods in printed sources, but I tried the following with satisfactory results. Place the disc in a lukewarm oven between two pieces of plate glass each ¼-inch thick and larger than the disc. Turn the oven off and allow the disc and pieces of glass to cool down in the oven undisturbed until the oven and its contents reach room temperature. Jaffe claims that

> Records warped by careless storage may be restored to their original condition by simply placing them back in the record rack, between other records, and waiting a few weeks to a few months, depending on the severity of the wrap.[2]

Protective Covering. Attractive and/or informative slipcases should be protected by transparent durable covers because most slipcases will not stand up to constant handling. Inexpensive covers are available commercially.

Discs should be stored within slipcases in polyethylene liners. Many producers package discs in liners suitable for storage. However, paper or glassine inner liners should be discarded unless they are acid-free. Watch especially for poor quality paper which can shed paper dust. The cost of replacing liners is low.

Cleanliness. A clean disc has a longer life and greater fidelity. Staff should resist the temptation to blow on discs to remove dust because particles contained in breath moisture may be deposited. Many aids for cleaning discs are available commercially including equipment attachments, mechanical devices, and chemical solutions. Some cleaning devices, such as silicone-treated cloths, must be changed frequently to ensure that dust and dirt are not being redeposited.

There is a controversy among experts over the efficacy and safety of washing sound discs in distilled water and liquid detergent. The discs in a circulating collection will need regular cleaning because they may be handled by careless users on improperly maintained equipment. Library staff members should experiment by washing discs in a certain section of the collection and judging the results before investing in more expensive methods. Several citations in Further Reading at the end of this chapter and in the General Bibliography give instructions on washing techniques. Unfortunately, the authors differ somewhat on the proper method.

The risk of dust contamination will be reduced if the opening of the polyethylene liner is at a 90° angle to the opening of the slipcase. This has the additional benefit of holding the disc more securely in the slipcase, decreasing the possibility of the disc falling out accidentally.

The disc surface and the stylus should not be touched because the body oils deposited will attract dust and provide areas hospitable to the growth of mold. Only the rim and the label should be touched. Figure 5 shows the placement of the thumb and fingers when handling the disc. Discs should not be rubbed or slid along any surface. When removing a disc from its slipcase, the sides of the slipcase should be bowed to admit the easy insertion of a hand or the disc should be pulled out by a corner of the inner sleeve. If the slipcase is too narrow, the disc should be removed with the aid of a clean piece of lintless cloth or gloves. A lintless cloth should also be used to remove any fingermarks found on improperly handled discs.

The turntable mat should be covered with a thin polyethylene disc which can be purchased or cut from a spare inner liner. This will help to keep discs clean because the mat cover can be wiped with a barely damp lintless cloth before use, thus removing any dust which might be on the turntable.

The polyethylene mat cover has a second function; it indicates the presence of static build-up, which attracts dust. If the sound disc is carrying

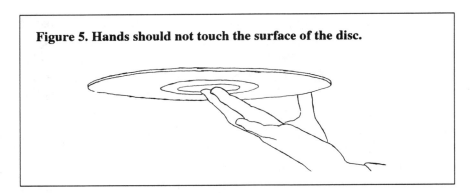

Figure 5. Hands should not touch the surface of the disc.

a static charge, the polyethylene mat cover will stick to its underside. The degree to which the polyethylene clings to the sound disc gives some indication of the strength of the charge. Anti-static agents should be used to eliminate static build-up; works in Further Reading at the end of this chapter and in the General Bibliography discuss various ways of accomplishing this. An easy temporary method of discharging static is to wipe a disc with a barely damp, soft, lintless cloth.

Damage Record. Some commercially available album covers have diagrams on which damage to the disc can be recorded. Even if a library does not require patrons to be financially responsible for damage, the notations about damage may make borrowers more careful of the discs in their care.

Storage

The ideal way to preserve discs is to lay each disc singly on a flat surface which provides equal support to all points. This is obviously impractical for a library because of the amount of space required. Discs cannot be piled horizontally one on top of the other because the pressure on the discs in the lower part of the pile causes warping and surface imprinting. Therefore, library collections should be shelved vertically. It is best to have discs in a fully vertical position because off-vertical stacking can cause warp. When patrons borrow discs, enough space may be created in the shelving to allow discs to tilt. This can be corrected by having temporary blocks available which can be placed in the space until the discs are returned. On the other hand, discs should not be stored so tightly that shelving and retrieval causes grinding. The ideal for vertical storage is to have enough pressure exerted on the discs to keep them erect, but still be able to remove them with relative ease.

In busy circulating collections off-vertical stacking, e.g., browser bins, may not be a problem because discs may not sit in one spot long enough to warp and public convenience may be a higher priority than disc durability. Bins should not be filled to the point where patrons can cause damage by trying to see titles on discs that cannot be flipped easily. On the other hand, off-vertical stacking should be avoided in those sections of the collection that circulate infrequently.

Bins must be designed so that discs will not be able to slip under other discs, thus causing damage. The bin should have a nonskid bottom, such as a grooved rubber pad, and its construction should not allow discs to lean too far backward or forward.

Intershelving of Sound Discs

Boxes. Most commercially produced albums in boxed sets can be intershelved. Sturdy boxes specifically designed to house sound discs are available commercially for those items received without boxes or in inadequate boxes. If needed, inserts can be placed in the boxes to hold the discs in a vertical position. Boxes shelved in situations where they might fall over can be placed in clip-on holders discussed below (see Figure 19a later in Chapter 7).

Clip-on Holders. Tall, narrow clip-on holders are self-supporting and will allow sound discs to be housed in a vertical position in the proper classification sequence on the shelf. Their width, generally slightly under two inches, provides assurance that, after some discs have been removed for circulation, the remaining discs will tilt only slightly. The information on the spine of the slipcase can be seen and the disc is readily available for circulation (see Figure 34g later in Chapter 9).

A general description of clip-on holders can be found in Chapter 4.

Freestanding Containers. This method of storing sound discs was developed by the Library of Congress as part of a research study on archival collections.[3] The Library of Congress recommends that twenty 12-inch discs be housed in a cardboard container. One end of the container is open to display the information on the spine of the slipcase and to allow easy access to the discs.

This convenient and economical storage system is well suited to circulating multimedia collections. The containers can be shelved in the appropriate place in the classification system and the size of the containers adapted to varying storage needs. Care must be taken to ensure that the cardboard in the containers is strong enough to maintain the discs in a fully vertical position. If a container houses only one or two discs, either permanently or temporarily, blocks can be placed in the spaces to keep the disc(s) vertical. A local box manufacturer may be able to supply this type of container in appropriate sizes quite inexpensively.

Freestanding units made of transparent rigid plastic are also available commercially. These have an interlocking device if greater capacity is needed. They are more expensive and have less potential for flexibility than cardboard containers (see Figure 28d later in Chapter 8).

Partial Intershelving of Sound Discs

Multimedia Shelf with Movable Spacing Panels. Vertical stacking in compartments separated by fixed spacing panels 3½ to 4 inches apart is recommended for archival storage. This can be adapted to circulating collections by having the end of a regular shelf fitted with movable spacing panels. If the library staff includes a good carpenter, the cost of such shelving adaptations will be low (see Figure 6e).

Multimedia Shelf with Pull-Out Rack or Bin. Sound discs may be housed in bins or racks on sliding tracks which are attached to one end of a shelf (see Figure 7h). The bin or rack is pulled out for easy access; when

---

Figure 6. Multimedia shelf with movable spacing panels.

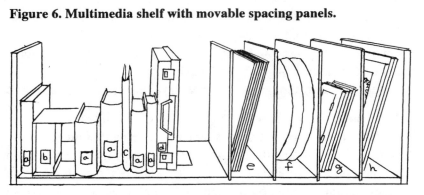

a. book; b. microfilm or motion picture loop cartridge in a stacking module; c. pamphlet binder containing two-dimensional material in a binder page; d. slide file; e. sound discs; f. motion pictures in film cans; g. transparencies; h. pictures

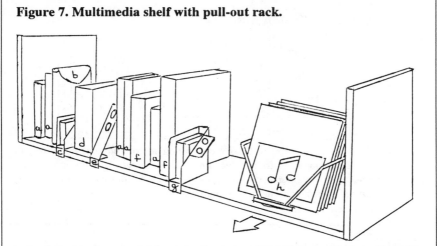

Figure 7. Multimedia shelf with pull-out rack.

a. book; b. envelope containing two-dimensional materials; c. clip-on holder with small slide box; d. book-like album containing slides and manual; e. clip-on filmstrip holder; f. box containing kit; g. clip-on sound cassette and filmstrip holder; h. sound discs on pull-out rack

not in use, the unit is pushed back so that its front is flush, or almost flush, with the rest of the shelf. The decision to use bins or racks is based on whether public convenience or disc durability is given priority; bins allow better accessibility, racks hold discs in a more vertical position.

Multimedia Shelf with Commercial Rack. This is probably the easiest and cheapest method of partial intershelving for sound discs. Racks are available at a low price in most stores that sell sound discs. A rack placed on one end of a shelf holds discs with their spines facing the public (see Figure 8g). Many racks can be purchased in, or cut to, appropriate sizes. The racks can be readily moved unless the library has had the racks attached to the shelves for greater stability. Racks should not be filled tightly and wire dividers should be sufficiently high to properly support discs.

A general description of racks is found in Chapter 4.

Hanging Devices. Some of the hanging bags discussed in Chapter 4 are large enough to accommodate 12-inch or smaller discs. The bags do not provide support or protection for easily damaged items; discs should be stored by this method only when they are not crowded and subject to pressure. Albums and well-packaged single discs are better suited to this type of storage (see Figure 9).

Figure 8. Multimedia shelf with rack.

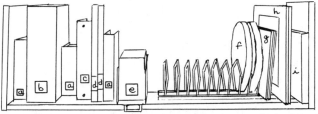

a. book; b. diorama in box; c. binder containing microcomputer cassettes; d. pamphlet binder containing folded two-dimensional material; e. motion picture loop cartridge and container in clip-on holder; f. motion picture reel in container; g. sound disc in slipcase; h. pictures; i. game in box

Figure 9. Hanging bags.

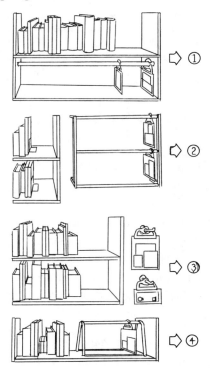

1. full shelf storage; 2. bars for hanging bags mounted on wall beside appropriate classification; 3. utility brackets for hanging bags mounted on wall beside appropriate classification; 4. free-standing racks for hanging bags placed on shelf at end of appropriate classification sequence

Cartmobiles. Cartmobiles containing racks for sound discs are used where shelf space is limited. A general description of cartmobiles is found in Chapter 4 (see Figure 10).

Figure 10. Cartmobile with racks.

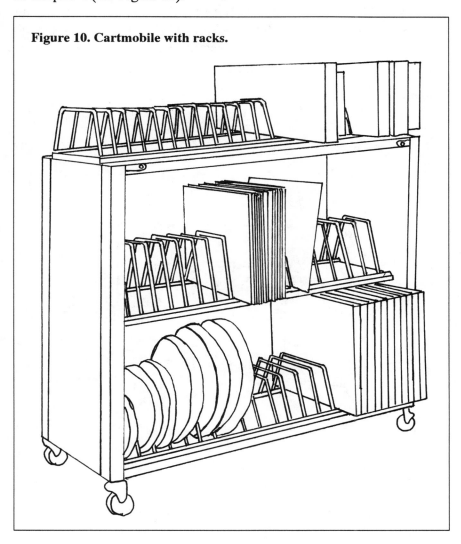

Mobile Bins. Where there are many sound discs in a classification sequence, e.g., 780s, and little shelf space, properly constructed mobile bins may house sound discs. Two types are available. One type has bins in both the upper and lower spaces; the other type has a bin in the upper space and an adjustable shelf for other materials below it (see Figure 11). These mobile bins should be placed near the appropriate shelves.

Figure 11. Mobile bin.

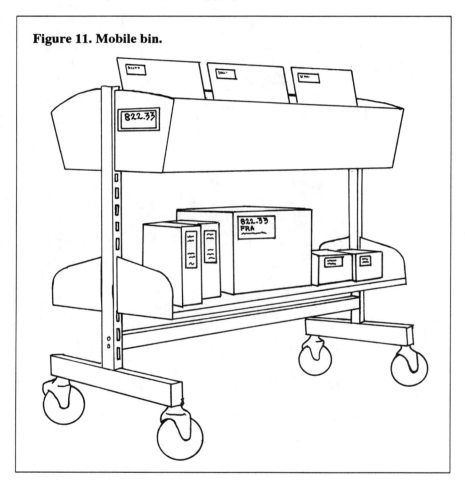

References

1. Andrew Pollack, "The End is Near for Vinyl Record," *Globe and Mail* (April 5, 1990). Reprinted from the New York Times Service.

2. Lee David Jaffe, "Phonograph Records" In *Nonbook Media: Collection Management and User Services*, edited by John W. Ellison and Patricia Ann Coty. (Chicago: American Library Association, 1987): p. 253.

3. A.G. Pickett and M.M. Lemcoe, *Preservation and Storage of Sound Recordings*, (Washington, DC: Library of Congress, 1959), pp. 41–42.

Further Reading

Alexandrovich, George. "Keeping It Clean: Record Hygiene." *Stereo Review*. 42 (6) (June 1979): 78–81.

The results of stylus and disc wear and disc cleaning are examined using a scanning electron microscope.

Gagnon, Ronald. "Keep Record Collections in Tune." *Library Journal*. 110 (19) (November 15, 1985): 56–58.

Practical suggestions for analog sound disc care, cleaning, and control of static electricity, dust, and warping.

Rosenberg, Kenyon C., with the assistance of Feinstein, Paul T. *Dictionary of Library and Educational Technology*. 2nd ed., rev. and expanded. Littleton, CO: Libraries Unlimited, 1983.

On page 13 the authors claim "getting rid of static charge is rather simple" and describe a method of attaching aluminum foil to the turntable mat.

Vaughan, Ted W. "How to Care for Your Records." *Instructional Innovator*. 29 (3) (March 1984): 38, 40.

Chapter 6
Magnetic Tapes
(Computer Tapes, Sound
Tapes, Videotapes)

Audiovisual equipment has become part of everyday life in many homes, and this is reflected in the demands made on libraries. Many librarians and media specialists report that videocassettes are the fastest growing part of their collections. It has been estimated that on an average a videocassette is circulated 3½ to 4 times more than a popular fiction book.[1] This is not surprising since one or two videocassettes can be viewed in an evening while few of us can read a book in the same time span. Analog sound cassettes are also increasingly popular due, no doubt, to the Walkman and the car tape deck.

These two formats are likely to be in most multimedia collections and are, therefore, emphasized in this chapter. Some collections may contain reel-to-reel sound tapes or have older formats that have died or are dying, such as sound cartridges or microcomputer cassettes and cartridges.

Libraries may house two newer formats in future. Sony hopes that a cassette holding an 8-mm videotape will become as popular as the Walkman. As more prerecorded cassettes come on the market, libraries may be pressured to include them in their collections. Digital audiotapes, frequently called DATs, and their equipment are still too expensive to engender public demand. If prices fall and prerecorded tapes are widely available, this format may also find a place in libraries.

Computer tapes that are part of research and specialized collections and broadcast and industrial standard videotapes are not usually found in libraries with open circulation policies. Although this chapter does not deal with these tapes, or the 8-mm videocassette, or DATs, some of the content may be applied to these formats.

Care and Handling

Cleanliness. It is essential to keep magnetic tape as dust-free as possible because dust can cause dropouts and sound distortion. Tapes should be kept in containers when not in use, and those not in cassettes or cartridges should be placed in polyethylene bags sealed with tape or with the edges of the bag folded over. Dust must be removed from all parts of an empty reel before use. Playback equipment should be clean and heads demagnetized periodically to prevent a build-up of static electricity which attracts dust. One play on a dirty, maladjusted machine could possibly destroy a tape that otherwise has been handled and stored properly. Some libraries keep supplies of sound cassette cleaning tapes and encourage borrowers to use them on their home equipment. These cleaning tapes have an effective life of 10–25 uses. Before initiating such a policy, a study should be made of various cleaning tape brands to select one that does an effective job without harming equipment.

As with sound analog discs, tape should never be touched because oil from fingermarks deposited on the tape holds dust. If tape must be handled (for example in splicing), lintless gloves must be worn. A long leader tape at the beginning and end of the magnetic tape will ensure that only the leader is handled during threading. In addition, leader tape will reduce the stress on the main tape when the end of the reel is reached in high speed transport. It also allows frayed and wrinkled ends, which may cause uneven winds and damage recorder heads, to be removed without jeopardizing any recorded material. The free end of the tape should be secured with an appropriate pressure-sensitive tape.

Reels and Cassette Shells. Bent, chipped, cracked, split, warped, or otherwise damaged reels should be replaced. Large reels should be handled and carried by the hub rather than the flange because a bent flange can damage the tape. The reel is removed from the transport by putting both hands as far around the back of the reel as possible. Do not push or pull the flanges or squeeze the tape.

Warped cassette shells may cause reels to rub against the tape. Shells that have been secured with screws are replaced easily and are preferred to shells sealed with glue which are more difficult to repair.

Distortion and Erasure of Information. One of the greatest dangers to magnetic tapes, and one easily overlooked by library staff, is accidental erasure through exposure to magnetic fields. Metal shelves can conduct magnetic fields and should be grounded. There have been reports of wiring in walls creating a magnetic field that erased portions of a tape nearest the wall. Magnetic fields that can emanate from air conditioners, transformers, motors, generators, bulk erasers, photocopiers, speakers, computers, telephones, electric pencil sharpeners, fluorescent lamp fixtures, and other electric or electronic equipment may cause erasure. Fortunately, this problem occurs only in the vicinity of the magnetic field and depends on the strength of the field. Experts disagree about the amount of separation from the field needed—from 3 inches to 2 yards. Even the larger number can be easily accommodated in a library situation. Videotapes may suffer damage if placed on top of or beside a color television set in operation because the magnetic fields associated with some components of the set may cause erasure of recorded signals. If, for some reason, an item must be in the vicinity of a magnetic field, it may be wrapped in aluminum foil to reduce the possibility of erasure from the field; plastic and paper do not protect enclosed material from magnetic erasure.

Accidental erasure is no longer a problem with most security systems. Many manufacturers have developed methods that allow a magnetic tape to be passed through their systems without danger to the tape.

Accidental erasure of tape content may also result if the recording function of the equipment is on during playback. This can be avoided by ensuring that the control tab, button, or switch which permits recording is removed or turned off. Heavily used equipment should be demagnetized according to manufacturers' instructions after 10 hours of playback.

Vibrations can cause dropout or distortion in videotape. Videotapes should not be stored in an area where these are likely to occur.

Magnetic tape should be placed neither on top of equipment in operation nor on equipment that has not cooled. For example, the heat generated by a sound tape machine may cause a temperature of 150°F/65°C, which is significantly higher than the 80°F/27°C recommended as the upper temperature limit for good magnetic tape care. Heat can cause print-through in which one layer of tape transmits some of its information to an adjacent layer. Prompt removal of the tape from the machine at the end of the playback will decrease the chance of heat-induced print-through.

Tape left in a nonoperating machine for days promotes the risk of damage to the exposed section of a tape from humidity, dust, and other contaminants and to the tape heads because high humidity can cause a tape to leave a sticky residue.

Lack of use can cause print-through. Experts' recommendations about how often unused tapes should be played vary from six months to two years.

The proper winding and rewinding of tape is important because ridges or buckling may be the result of incorrect tension: ridges indicate too high, and buckling too low, tension. Creased or damaged tapes should not be played because this can result in head wear or damage. Damage to heads and to videotapes is also possible when the pause button on equipment is used for more than a minute or two.

Security Considerations. Libraries in communities where theft is a problem must take action to secure their collections. Labels can be removed by the unscrupulous; it is much more difficult, and perhaps impossible to remove a name engraved on a cassette shell. An indelible ink symbol can be placed down the wells of tape hubs. In some thefts homemade copies are substituted for the original. In order to discourage this type of theft, some libraries affix adhesive labels over the seam that seals the two halves of the cassette shell. One such method is described:

> To prevent video pirates from substituting homemade copies for original VHS videocassettes, the Edmonton (Alta.) Public Library Book Processing and Printing Division has devised a tamper-proof method. Checkpoint security labels are now sealed in Destrux P-5 labels, custom-made for the library by Avery. Destrux P-5 is made from a material that doesn't peel off cleanly. A smaller Destrux warning label is placed on the seam of the videocassette to alert staff if the cassette has been tampered with, and another Destrux label, recording title and ownership, is placed in the center.[2]

Labels. 3M warns that videocassette shells are designed with specific areas to which labels are to be affixed and that labels placed elsewhere may cause a cassette to jam in the player. Jamming can result also from a build-up of labels; therefore, old labels should be removed before new ones are applied.

Repairs. Resist the impulse to insert a pointed instrument into a cassette that is not operating as it should. Avoid lifting the flap on a videocassette to see what is wrong. Do not touch unwound tape with your fingers. Many problems can be fixed easily; for example, a cassette shell or leader tape can be replaced or tape rewound properly, if the problem is not worsened by "fiddling."

If a damaged tape must be copied, use a major brand of videotape. Consumer Reports' tests on VHS tapes indicate that these tapes "have attained a high plateau of performance . . . that differences between best and worst were barely noticeable" and that "there is little difference between major brands of VHS tape." They warn that "off-brand tapes . . . including 'private label' products that carry the store's name . . . may not meet the tape manufacturing standards."[3] Research by the Canadian Association of Consumers produced the same results.[4]

Storage

All storage devices should be large enough to accommodate a container that houses a tape, cassette, or cartridge because the container provides necessary protection from dust and dirt. Some commercial storage units for sound and videocassettes will not hold a container; these should be avoided unless they have a dust-tight closure.

Magnetic tapes should be stored vertically with the loaded hub below the empty hub because horizontal stacking can cause reel shape distortions in the lower part of the stack which, in turn, may damage the tape.

There is controversy over whether tapes should be stored in a "just played" state or whether they should be stored rewound. There is agreement, however, that a tape should never be rewound at high speed or stored half wound. Some people advocate "just played" storage because a tape is not under as much tension as it is after rewinding. Those who advocate rewinding believe that a tape played to the end will not be unevenly wound, and a rewound tape is more convenient for the patron. Some libraries prefer that a tape be returned unwound so that the rewinding can be done properly by library staff who will, at the same time, check for problems and damage. One specialist insists that sound cassettes be returned fully rewound so that library staff will be able to detect easily a tape that has been damaged. It will be impossible for a borrower to rewind a broken or jammed tape, and the matt surface of a twisted tape will be visible. He suggests that library staff at the same time also watch for damage to the cassette shell and for telltale signs of tampering, such as a sticky residue on the cassette shell which may indicate that recording prevention openings have been closed.

Intershelving of Magnetic Tape

Many videotapes can be successfully intershelved in the containers in which they have been received from commercial producers because these containers have been constructed so that the videotape is supported by the hub rather than the flange. Such containers are available commercially if needed. In order to save time processing title labels for opaque containers, purchased containers should be transparent, enabling patrons to read the label on the cassette and thereby reducing unnecessary handling. On the other hand, if videocassettes are received in informative, but insubstantial, containers, the containers should be covered and strengthened with transparent plastic film. Easy to apply, adhesive videocassette box covers cut to size are available commercially at reasonable prices. Another way to preserve insubstantial, attractive video jackets is to purchase containers that accommodate a videocassette with its jacket. The video jacket is secured inside the box by a flange and the cassette is extracted from the bottom of the container.

Reel-to-reel sound tapes in sturdy boxes are also easy to intershelve. Sound and microcomputer cassettes and cartridges present a shelving challenge due to their size.

If a particular area of a library is subject to vibrations, a dummy block or a browser card should be placed at the appropriate point on the shelf telling patrons where an item is housed.

Book-like Albums. Albums are available commercially for sound and videocassettes (see Figures 1d, 3, 12, and later, in Chapter 9, Figure 34b). Those for sound cassettes provide one answer to the danger of small-size cassettes being lost on the shelves. Marketed in different sizes, they are able to house a varying number of cassettes; many such albums have space for accompanying manuals. Albums that accommodate a cassette container or that have a dust-tight closure are preferred.

Albums are useful for videocassettes when a cassette has been received in a cardboard container that will not stand up to library use or when a cassette is accompanied by material that is to be used, and should be stored, with it. These albums, made for one or two cassettes with or without space for accompanying materials, have dust-tight closures. Cheap book-like albums made of pressboard are not dust-tight and should only be used if a videocassette container can be accommodated within the album.

A general discussion of book-like albums is found in Chapter 4.

Figure 12. Book-like albums for sound or microcomputer cassettes housed with and without containers.

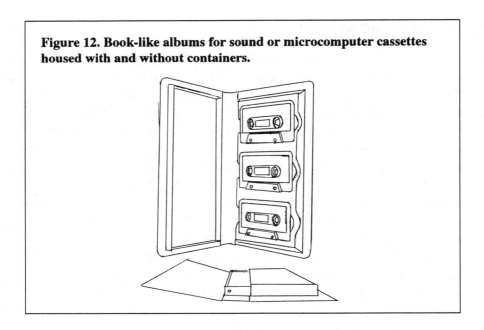

Boxes and Pamphlet Boxes. Boxes and pamphlet boxes are particularly, but not exclusively, useful for sets containing seven or more sound cassettes (see Figure 13). Pamphlet boxes rather than Princeton files are used for sound cassettes because the solid sides keep the cassettes well contained. Boxes may be homemade or purchased. Commercial corrugated cardboard boxes with inserts to hold cassettes are inexpensive and are available in different sizes. If a library has sound cassettes without cassette containers, storage in plastic bags which are then placed in closed containers may partially solve the dust problem.

Pamphlet boxes and Princeton files can only accommodate two videocassettes. Items consisting of three or more videocassettes may be housed in boxes.

A general discussion about boxes is found in Chapter 4.

Binders. Sound cassettes can be placed in the plastic "pages" of a binder (see Figures 8c and 14). Preference should be given to plastic pages that can accommodate the cassette container. However, if only the type of sound cassette page illustrated in Figure 14 is available, it can be inserted in a commercial or homemade transparent page normally associated with two-dimensional materials. This will provide protection against dirt and dust.

Figure 13. Commercial boxes for sound tapes are available in different sizes and materials.

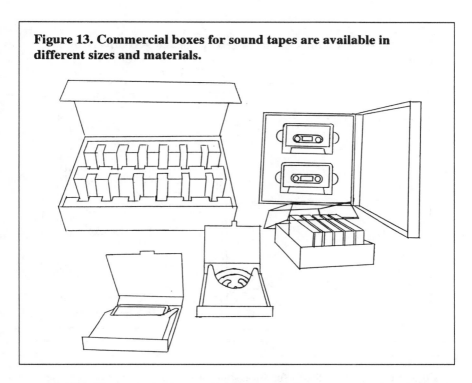

Similar binders are also available for videocassettes. Three-ring-hole molded pages accommodate one or two videocassettes and accompanying material is held in a pocket on the binder's inside cover. Generally, these binders do not have dust-tight closures; the transparent pages mentioned above to protect sound cassettes are not large enough to fit videocassettes. Unless a library wishes to make protective covers for each page, another type of videocassette container is preferred.

Clip-on Holders. Reel-to-reel sound tapes, sound cassettes, and microcomputer cassettes can be housed in clip-on holders (see Figures 7g and 15a). The bigger holders will accommodate sets containing a limited number of pieces. The storage in the same unit of a number of cassettes which do not belong to one set should be avoided, because some cassettes will be pushed to the back, away from the notice of the browser.

Small holders are preferred for single items and two or three component sets. These shallow units will hold small items at the front of the shelf.

A general description of clip-on holders is found in Chapter 4.

Figure 14. Binder with a sound cassette page and accompanying printed material.

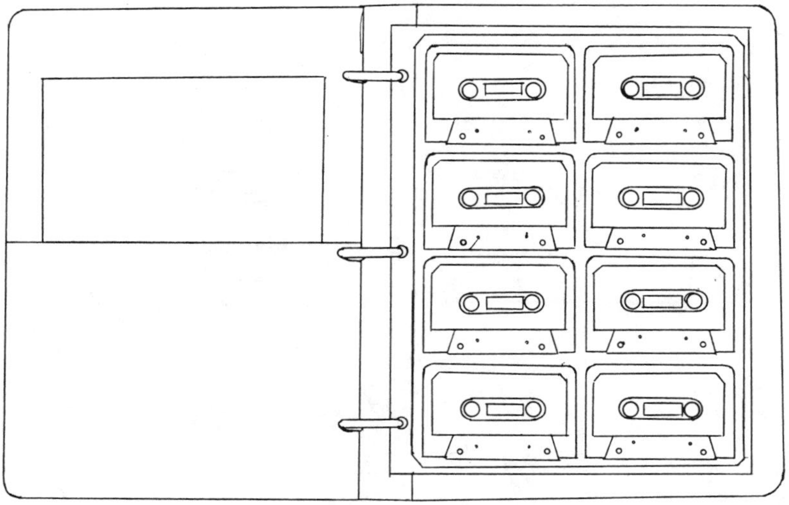

Figure 15. Some methods for intershelving sound tapes in which the individual labels are displayed.

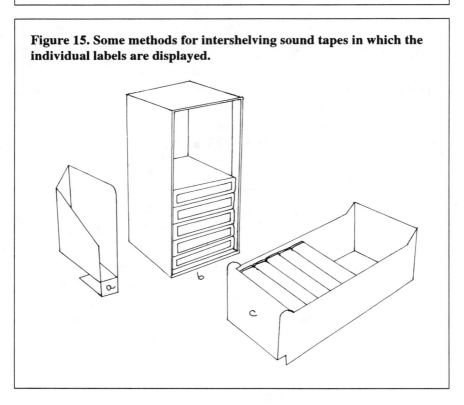

Modular Units. There are several manufacturers selling inexpensive modules with one open side that permits browsing for either cassettes or cartridges. Some modules can be stacked with an interlocking device if greater capacity is needed.

These units provide another method of holding small cassettes and cartridges at the front of the shelf; they can accommodate a larger set than clip-on holders (see Figures 15b and 16).

A general description of modular units is found in Chapter 4.

Trays. Trays which house cassettes or cartridges may be less satisfactory than other storage methods because the labels on the cassettes or cartridges at the back of the tray may be difficult to read without removing the tray from the shelf (see Figure 15c).

Figure 16. Interlocking modular units for sound tapes.

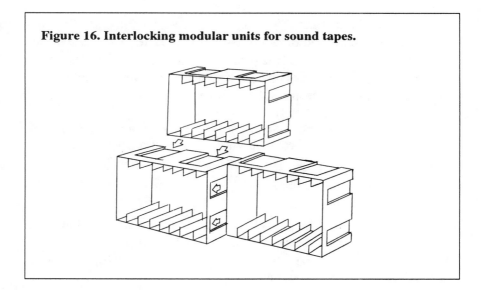

Partial Intershelving of Magnetic Tapes

Shelf with Commercial Rack. Racks designed to hold the various formats of magnetic tapes can be purchased and placed on one end of a shelf, or, if numbers warrant, a shelf-sized rack can be placed at the end of a particular classification sequence. Racks similar to the one illustrated in Figure 8 can house videotapes and cassettes; smaller racks are available for sound cassettes and cartridges.

Less satisfactory is a rack standing outside the shelves because it removes the materials even farther away from their place in the general classification scheme. Such a rack should only be used when a library (a) already possesses the rack, (b) has a large number of cassettes in one general classification, e.g., the 780s, (c) can place the rack very close to the shelves containing other items with this classification.

Hanging Devices. These devices, described in Chapter 4, provide flexible storage which will accommodate cassettes, cartridges, and reel-to-reel tapes (see Figure 9).

Separate Media Shelves. Cassettes, cartridges, and small reel-to-reel sound tapes can be housed on the media shelves described in Chapter 4 (see Figure 4d & i).

Mobile Browser Bins. The mobile bins described in Chapter 5 may also be used for sound and/or videocassettes in libraries with limited shelf space. In libraries where theft is a problem, surrogates with descriptive information may be placed in bins located near appropriate sections of the classification system. The surrogates can be:

- Attractive, descriptive containers, in which the items were marketed, which are flattened and covered with adhesive transparent film. This film, cut to an appropriate size, is available commercially.

- Browser cards made by library staff or volunteers from material cut out of producers' catalogs/brochures from which the items were ordered.

- Special plastic holders, marketed by some companies, into which such descriptive information can be inserted. The holders preserve the information from the hazards of much handling and provide a rigid surface to flip while browsing in the bins.

- Cataloging copy in computer print-out or catalog card format affixed to cardboard. This is more effective when the catalog record has a summary.

References

1. *The Librarian's Video Primer: Establishing and Maintaining Your Video Collection*, produced by the Georgia Library Video Association with Videoworks (Chicago: ALA Video, 1988). Videocassettes (VHS, Beta, 3/4 inch).

2. Iolani Domingo, "Action Exchange," *American Libraries*, vol. 18, no. 10 (November 1987): 830

3. "Videotapes," *Consumer Reports*, vol. 55, no. 9 (September 1990): 584–85.
4. "Videotapes." *Canadian Consumer*, vol. 20, no. 10 & 11 (1990): 8–10.

Further Reading

"Audio Cassette Tapes." *Canadian Consumer*. 19 (2) (1990): 29–33.
An evaluation of commercially available blank cassette tapes.

Barkholz, Gerald R. "Audiotapes." In *Nonbook Media: Collection Management and User Services*, edited by John W. Ellison and Patricia Ann Coty, pp. 20–31. Chicago: American Library Association, 1987.

Basic Tips on Video. Fairfax, Va: National Audiovisual Association, [19--]. Free.
This pamphlet includes concise recommendations about videocassette and VCR care and maintenance and the selection of equipment.

Bolnick, Doreen, and Johnson, Bruce. "Audiocassette Repair." *Library Journal.* 114 (19) (November 15, 1989): 43–46.
An illustrated, step-by-step guide to simple repairs, with a list of requirements for a cassette repair kit.

"Edmonton Library Devises Tamper-Proof Processing for VHS." *Alberta Library News.* 16 (2) (Fall/Winter 1987): 8.
Destrix P-5 labels are used to secure evidence of ownership.

Havens, Shirley E.; DeCandido, GraceAnne A.; and Fox, Bette-Lee. "Audio- & Videocassettes: Patron Demand = Library Response." *Library Journal.* 112 (19) (November 15, 1987): 33–35.
A survey of 80 academic, public, and special libraries in the US concerning circulation policies, acquisitions budgets, problems, etc. of cassettes.

Klein, Larry. "Tape Expectations." *High Fidelity.* 38 (3) (March 1988): 17.
A practical, well-balanced, brief discussion of videocassette care, handling, and storage.

Lora, Pat. "AV Frontier: Gold in my Junk Mail . . . and Other Discoveries!" *Wilson Library Bulletin.* 64 (10) (June 1990): 105–06, 173.
A description of devices for a browsable video collection—transparent video box containers, slatwall panels and units, label guns, category labels—all found through junk mail ads.

"Old & Dirty Videotapes Can Damage VCR Players." *Library Hotline.* 17 (16) (April 25, 1988): 5.
A warning that tapes played over 200 times can leave a powder damaging to video heads and a recommendation that a statement disclaiming responsibility should be affixed to all tapes circulated.

Research Technology International. *The Videotape Cassette Care Handbook.* Lincolnwood, IL: RTI, 1987.
This booklet gives brief advice on care, handling, and storage.

Saddington, George H., and Cooper, Eric. *Audiocassettes as Library Materials: An Introduction.* 2nd rev. ed. London: Audiovisual Librarian, 1984.
Includes the care, handling, and repair of sound cassettes and a brief discussion of storage units with a list of British manufacturers.

Schabert, Daniel R. "Videotapes." In *Nonbook Media: Collection Management and User Services*, edited by John W. Ellison and Patricia Ann Coty, pp. 361–76. Chicago: American Library Association, 1987.

Schenck, Thomas. "Magnetic Tape Care, Storage, and Error Recovery." *Library Hi Tech.* 2 (4) (1984): 51–54.
Much of this discussion about the care, handling, and storage of computer tape reels can also be applied to all magnetic tapes.

Scholz, James C. *Developing and Maintaining Video Collections in Libraries.* Santa Barbara, CA: ABC-CLIO, 1989.
This well-illustrated, practical work includes a discussion of storage options, repair techniques, cleaning devices, diagrams for the construction of storage units, anti-theft devices, and sources of supply.

Utz, Peter. *Do-It-Yourself Video: A Beginner's Guide to Home Video.* Englewood, NJ: Prentice-Hall, 1984.
This breezily written book includes basic information about the care and handling of videotapes and recorders.

"Videotapes, Standard, High-Grade, Hi-Fi, Professional: Besides Price, What's the Difference?" *Consumer Reports.* 53 (9) (September 1988): 583–86.
This evaluation of 27 videotapes available in the US marketplace includes brief guidelines for care, handling, and storage and a paragraph on how to recognize unlicensed tapes.

Williams, Gene "The VCR in the Library: Tips on Care and Maintenance." *Wilson Library Bulletin.* 61 (2) (October 1986): 14–17.
A nontechnical explanation of internal VCR operations and remedies for operating problems, VCR cleaning, and videocassette repair. Includes a troubleshooting chart.

Youkhana, David. *Do It Yourself on How to Maintain and Clean Your Own VCR.* Chicago: American Gifts [distributor], 1988.
Illustrated step-by-step instructions for basic repairs and cleaning.

Chapter 7
Film Media (Filmstrips, Microforms, Motion Pictures, Slides, Transparencies)

Despite their different formats, all film media have many common guide-lines for care and handling. The first section of this chapter deals with these common features. This is followed by sections devoted to the specific requirements for storage and, in some cases, care and handling of the separate film formats. The contents of this chapter are concerned with service copies; master copies should be preserved in archival conditions.

Photographs are not included in this chapter because most multimedia libraries do not circulate them. Some specific works about their care, handling, and storage are found at the end of the General Bibliography.

Care and Handling

Handling Film. All film formats should be handled only at the edges, by the mounts, or by leader and end tapes. As with other nonbook materials, the oil and bacteria from fingerprints can cause deterioration and attract dust and dirt. The fingerprint itself is difficult to remove and will show on the item when it is projected. If touching the surface is unavoidable, clean lintless gloves should be worn.

Care should be taken not to twist or cinch film when handling. For example, the temptation to pull on the end of a filmstrip in order to fit it into a canister must be resisted because such cinching will cause scratches. Cinch marks may also appear if the film is dropped or jarred.

Film should be wound evenly in a tight roll without pulling. A roll which is not held firmly by its container should be fastened with a piece of special pressure-sensitive tape, an acid-free button-and-string tie, or a sulphur-free rubber band.

Cleanliness. All film media must be kept clean. There is disagreement about whether film can be manually cleaned by someone other than an expert and about various methods of cleaning film. These controversies can be explored by consulting Further Reading at the end of this chapter and the General Bibliography.

Dust is an enemy of film, for it not only detracts from the picture image during projection, but also causes film deterioration. Film should be stored in containers with lids that can be securely fastened, and equipment must be kept dust free. Do not blow on film to remove dust; moisture from the breath can condense on the film causing damage. A soft, dry brush or can of clean pressurized air is recommended for removing dust from surfaces.

Since static electricity attracts dust, it is wise to install anti-static carpeting or leave the floors bare in areas where film media are found. The chance of general static is lessened if floors are vacuumed rather than swept.

All film formats should be inspected after each use for dirt and damage, such as torn sprocket holes, weak splices, and tears. It is difficult to detect anything but the most obvious types of damage by manual inspection. Those libraries that do not have motion picture inspection machines and/or sufficient staff to inspect film media should encourage their patrons to report any damage or areas of trouble.

Some film experts recommend that film media be "photogarded" for added protection. Articles on this process are listed in Further Reading at the end of this chapter.

Heat and Humidity. Control of relative humidity in the environment is especially important for film. Dryness and dampness will both cause deterioration. An atmosphere with low humidity will result in brittle film which is easily destroyed. A damp sponge placed for a week with the film in an airtight container provides temporary relief by restoring brittle film, but the sponge must not touch the film.

On the other hand, high humidity encourages fungal growth and film base degeneration. The presence of Newton's Rings in slides indicates residual moisture and should alert the library to the possibility of high humidity levels. Silica gel placed in a container can be used to reduce moisture, but it must be replaced periodically for it is no longer effective once its saturation point has been reached. Still film media can be dried by projection; however, each exposure must be limited to 30 seconds to prevent heat and light damage. In areas of high or low humidity, air conditioning is the only permanent solution. It must be remembered that not all air conditioning controls humidity as well as temperature. When humidity control is important, the air conditioning system must be designed specifically for that purpose.

While containers should be securely fastened to prevent the entrance of dust, they should not be airtight; the circulation of air prevents moisture accumulation.

High temperatures also contribute to the general deterioration of film. Therefore, film media should be stored away from sources of heat such as radiators, steampipes, hot air ducts, air conditioners, direct sunlight, and bright lights.

Color dyes are particularly subject to fading. However, the Eastman Kodak Company advertises that color film can be expected to have a useful life of many years if the film is shown with care and good projection equipment. The heat generated inside a projector can cause both color and black-and-white film to warp or even to melt. If a slide mounted in glass is subjected to such heat, the film can adhere to the glass. Only projectors with adequate cooling systems should be purchased. Care should be taken to use the correct wattage in the projection bulb. A higher than necessary wattage will produce added heat. Projection should be limited to 30 seconds for each slide or filmstrip frame or for each use of the stop button on a motion picture projector during normal viewing, as well as for drying out a too-humid film. Slides should not be left on light boxes, nor microforms in their readers, for prolonged periods. Film must be brought to room temperature before viewing. Sudden large temperature changes put great stress on film.

Composition of Containers. Containers should be made of chemically stable plastic, or acid-free, lignin-free, unbuffered paper products, or nonferrous metals, because these materials will not react with the chemicals in film. Do not house film media in containers made of wood. It is usually safe to use the containers in which film media have been marketed because they are likely to be free of harmful ingredients.

Labels. Labels should not be affixed to film media because the adhesive may damage the film or the label may be caught in the equipment. Ownership identification can be added by film-marking pen.

Prohibited Storage. The Eastman Kodak Company recommends that film not be stored near the following: ammonia, cleaners, formaldehyde, fungicides and insecticides, hydrogen sulfide, mercury, mothballs, motor exhaust, paints, solvents, turpentine, and wood glues. Storage on open shelves usually permits enough ventilation to minimize potential problems.

Before an area is painted or if it is exposed to fumes of unknown composition, film media should be removed and not reshelved for a period of at least two weeks or preferably three months. The latter time period will ensure that film will be safe from exposure to harmful oxidizing contaminants.

Manufacturers should be able to guarantee that all their paper-based containers sold for film media have passed a photoactivity test.

Integral Magnetic Sound. Sound slides and motion pictures with magnetic sound tracks will be governed also by the additional considerations for the care, handling, and storage of magnetic tape found in Chapter 6.

Filmstrips

Storage

Filmstrip canisters are small, lightweight, and, therefore, not easily intershelved by themselves. They are frequently sold with accompanying manuals, with or without packaging. The filmstrip and manual should be stored together because a separately housed manual is more likely to be mislaid or lost, and the retrieval and shelving of separate parts involves twice as much work.

Filmslips are not included in this section because few libraries possess them. They should be treated in the same manner as filmstrips. Filmslips packaged in flat strips or produced in a rigid format are stored in the manner described for transparencies.

Intershelving of Filmstrips

Boxes and Pamphlet Boxes. Many filmstrips are sold in boxes suitable for intershelving (see Figures 1c, 17a, 18a and later, in Chapter 8, Figure 28f). If a filmstrip with or without an accompanying manual is received in unsuitable packaging, both can be housed in a homemade, purchased, or casually acquired box. Commercial corrugated cardboard boxes with inserts to hold canisters are inexpensive and available in different sizes with capacities that range from 1 to 30 filmstrips. Most boxes enclose the filmstrip canister(s); there are some that are designed to expose the canister label (see Figure 21a and later, in Chapter 8, Figure 28f).

Pamphlet boxes rather than Princeton files are used for filmstrips because the canister's small size requires the confinement of solid sides. Pamphlet boxes should not be used in libraries where shelving might be done carelessly, e.g., where there are young, exuberant shelvers, because a canister may roll or be bumped out of a pamphlet box.

A general discussion about boxes is found in Chapter 4.

Book-like Albums. Commercially produced book-like albums are available for single filmstrips or filmstrip sets. As with commercial boxes, some have windows or openings which allow the canister label to be seen (see Figure 17b and later, in Chapter 9, Figure 34a).

A general description of book-like albums is found in Chapter 4.

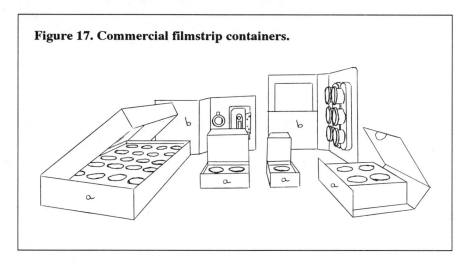

Figure 17. Commercial filmstrip containers.

Clip-on Filmstrip Canister Holders. The clip-on filmstrip holder is an effective device for libraries wishing to display canister labels (see Figures 7e and 18b & c). When holders are properly attached to the shelf, canisters are unlikely to fall out, yet they are easily removed. There are two types of holders, those that accommodate filmstrips only and those that house both filmstrip and manual. The holders are made with one, two, three, or four canister holes.

A general description of clip-on holders is found in Chapter 4.

Freestanding Filmstrip Canister Holders. Freestanding tilted canister holders are similar to clip-ons in that they allow display of filmstrip labels and provide easy access. The commercially available holders, usually made of cardboard-like materials, are suitable only for filmstrips without manuals. These holders could be made of wood easily and economically by an amateur carpenter, e.g., staff member, volunteer, shop class student. There are advantages to the homemade holder; the required number of holes can be drilled and storage can be attached for manuals when needed (see Figure 19b).

Trays. Trays with inserts to hold filmstrip sets may not be as satisfactory as some other methods of storage because they do not accommodate manuals, and the canister labels at the back of the tray may be difficult to read without removing the tray from the shelf (see Figure 18d).

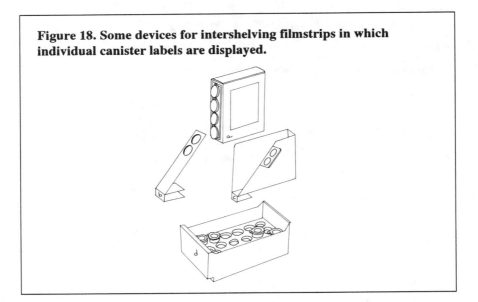

Figure 18. Some devices for intershelving filmstrips in which individual canister labels are displayed.

Partial Intershelving of Filmstrips

Hanging Devices. These devices, described in Chapter 4, can accommodate both filmstrips and manuals (see Figure 9).

Separate Media Shelf. Filmstrips without manuals can be housed on the media shelves (see Figure 4c) described in Chapter 4.

Figure 19. Freestanding tilted filmstrip holders used for total and partial intershelving.

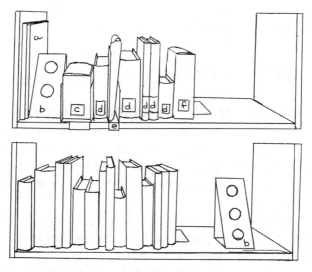

a. sound disc album in box; b. freestanding filmstrip canister holder; c. box containing microfilm placed in a clip-on holder; d. book; e. envelope containing two-dimensional material placed in a clip-on holder; f. microcomputer disks and manual in box

Slides

Storage

This section on slide storage presupposes that all slides in the collection are mounted since this is the way most slides are purchased or returned from the film processor. Information concerning the selection of suitable mounts is found in the works cited in Further Reading at the end of this chapter and in the General Bibliography.

Some of the storage methods described below necessitate the handling of slides for projection. It is possible to fit each slide with an individual sleeve that gives added protection during handling and projection. Slides that will be handled frequently should be remounted in glass slide bindings because dust and fingerprints can be removed easily. Slide binding should be done in a low-humidity area to decrease the chance of moisture entrapment. These measures, of course, raise the cost of storage and must be weighed against the replacement value of the slides.

Slides that are not circulated in slide trays or carousels and, therefore, will be loaded individually into patrons' projectors should have a thumbspot placed on each slide to indicate the positioning of the slide for proper loading.

Intershelving of Slides

Slide Trays and Carousels. Many slide sets are purchased or subsequently housed in slide trays/carousels that are designed to fit onto projection equipment. Some trays are received in boxes; others have storage lids. Both are easily intershelved (see Figures 1i and 20). This method of storage is best suited to slides that will be used as a set because individual slides are not readily located.

Before slides are inserted into a slide tray or carousel, a diagonal line may be drawn across the top edges of the slides from the first to the last slide in the set. When the slides are placed in a tray or carousel, it is easy to notice a break in the line that indicates a missing slide or one that is out of order. (See Figure 20.)

Slide trays and carousels are effective units for circulation because slides are housed in a manner that allows air to move freely around each slide and that affords physical protection from careless handling. Some libraries have adapted their slides trays and/or carousels so that only a staff member can insert or remove slides.

Boxes and Pamphlet Boxes. Boxes provided by manufacturers and processors make suitable storage containers because they are made of materials that will not harm the film. However, they are less than ideal for two reasons. First each slide must be handled before it can be browsed or used. Second, most of these boxes are small and, therefore, may be overlooked if they are inadvertently pushed to the back of the shelf. These small boxes can be placed in larger containers or in pamphlet boxes (see Figure 4j); this is a solution for those with generous shelving space.

Camera stores sell boxes for slide storage, generally called slide files. The majority are rectangular and can easily be intershelved by placing the slide file on its side (see Figure 6d) as long as it has a firm fastener that can withstand the hazards of shelving. Slide files have drawbacks, because each

Figure 20. Slide tray and carousel with diagonal line.

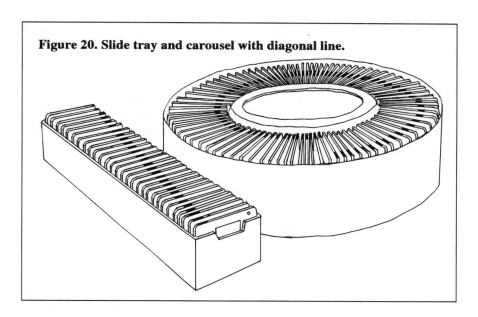

slide must be handled for any type of use. If individual slides, rather than sets, are housed, the file must be well labelled for the retrieval of each slide.

A general discussion about boxes is found in Chapter 4.

Clip-on Holders. Clip-on holders are another solution to the problem of small producers' boxes (see Figure 7c). Shallow holders will house these boxes at the front of the shelf. Tall, narrow clip-ons will accommodate plastic pages and envelopes of slides, giving support to those that cannot stand vertically by themselves.

A general description of clip-on holders is found in Chapter 4.

Binders. Slides can be housed in the pockets of transparent inert plastic pages inserted in a binder (see Figure 1f). Semi-rigid plastic will protect the slides better than soft plastic because the page neither bends as readily nor is as likely to touch the surface of the film. Some more expensive pages have pockets that are molded so that air can circulate around both sides of every slide, preventing moisture build-up. This method of storage allows easy intershelving and immediate browsing. However, slides must be handled for projection.

If the number of slides in a set is too large to be accommodated in a binder, the plastic pages can be housed in boxes, pamphlet boxes, or Princeton files.

A general description of binders is found in Chapter 4.

Book-like Albums. Book-like albums with permanently affixed boxes designed to hold slides are available (see Figure 7d). There are other albums that will hold slide carousels.

A general description of book-like albums is found in Chapter 4.

Envelopes. Single slides, Viewmaster, and other three-dimensional slides can be housed in acid-free, brightly colored manila envelopes (see Figure 1j). These envelopes can be intershelved or placed in the clip-on holders described above.

A general description of book-like albums is found in Chapter 4.

Partial Intershelving of Slides

Hanging Devices. Plastic sheets of slides, slides stored in small producers' boxes, and single slides in an envelope made of acid-free paper can be housed in a plastic bag and stored by the methods described in Chapter 4 (see Figure 9).

Separate Media Shelves. Only slides housed in small containers can be placed on the media shelves described in Chapter 4 (see Figure 4h).

Microforms

Most microforms do not circulate outside a library. This is changing somewhat as the number of users with access to readers increases and commercial rentals become available in urban centers. Some libraries loan portable microfiche readers to their patrons. Unfortunately, there appear to be no portable readers for microfilm. Libraries that cannot afford portable readers might consider small hand-held viewers, which are cheap, easy to use, and accommodate both film and fiche. These viewers are not very effective instruments, but they may fill a need for a patron who must use a microform outside the library.

Care and Handling

Microfilms. Open reels should not be filled because full reels are more difficult to handle, thereby increasing the possibility of damage. Microfilm should be stored on reels supplied by the manufacturer unless the reels are defective. If reels must be replaced or film is received without reels, microfilm should be placed on chlorine-free plastic reels.

Film on open reels is frequently secured with acid-free button-and-string ties. However, microfilm reels can be stored adequately without ties.

An 18-inch leader and tail will protect a microfilm against fingerprints, dust, and dirt.

Microfiches. Each microfiche should be housed in an acid-free, unbuffered paper envelope to protect the fiche and prevent it sticking to another fiche. A fiche should be placed in its envelope with the emulsion side away from interior seams to prevent abrasion and possible contact with adhesives. Plastic sleeves made of Mylar D, polyester, polyethylene, polypropylene, or polystyrene may also be used. There is debate among archivists whether paper or plastic enclosures are best for long-term storage. If proper temperature and humidity conditions can be maintained, it is possible, although not preferable, to store microfiches without individual envelopes.

Aperture Cards and Microopaques. Aperture cards and microopaques should be packed tightly so they will not warp. Acid-free inserts should be used in a container which is not full.

Intershelving of Microfilm Reels, Cartridges, and Cassettes

Boxes and Pamphlet Boxes. Most microfilms can be shelved in the boxes in which they are marketed. If these boxes are being pushed to the back of the shelf because of their small size, the stacking modules or clip-on holders described below will alleviate the problem.

Microfilm sets can be housed in boxes sized to appropriate dimensions (see Figure 11e), in pamphlet boxes, or in Princeton files.

A general discussion about boxes is found in Chapter 4.

Clip-on Holders. Small clip-ons will hold one or two microfilms at the front of the shelf (see Figure 19c).

A general description of clip-on holders is found in Chapter 4.

Modular Units. Another method of holding microfilm to the front of the shelf is the use of modular units, which have one open side for browsing (see Figure 6b). Most of these inexpensive modules can accommodate four 16-mm or two 35-mm microfilms. Many units, similar to the ones for sound tapes illustrated in Figure 16, have an interlocking device for stacking if greater capacity is needed.

A general description of modular units is found in Chapter 4.

Intershelving of Microfiches, Microopaques, and Aperture Cards

Boxes and Pamphlet Boxes. Some sets of fiches, opaques, and cards are received in containers suitable for shelving; others can be placed in boxes or pamphlet boxes of appropriate sizes. Princeton files can only be used for large items which will not drop out of the bottom openings (see Figure 11 and later, in Chapter 8, Figure 28c).

A general discussion about boxes is found in Chapter 4.

Binders. Many commercially made sheet microform storage containers were developed for the COM catalog. Most of these are ring or album-type binders with pages especially adapted for microfiches so that the fiche header can be read without removing the item (see Figures 1b and 21). The information on the fiche header may be easier to read if the binder is a different color than the fiche header.

This method of storage can also be used for microopaques and aperture cards if they are not too large to fit into the fiche pockets. The library staff could make pages for the larger items.

A general description of binders is found in Chapter 4.

Book-like Containers. Each sheet of a microfiche, microopaque, or aperture card set may be inserted into a separate pocket of a book-like container (see Figure 22). The number of pockets can be varied according to the size of the set. This container is easily intershelved.

Trays. Large sets of fiches, opaques, or cards may be housed in trays. The trays should be opaque and covered with lids to protect the contents from light sources.

Single Items. Many librarians will not want to waste space by housing a single item in a box or pamphlet box. The following are suggestions for storing the single microfiche, microopaque, or aperture card (see Figure 6c and later, in Chapter 9, Figure 34f):

1. The item can be housed in a large, brightly colored, acid-free envelope that is rigid enough for shelving.

2. The item can be housed in a binder page and the page placed in a pamphlet binder.

   Either of these methods permits intershelving.

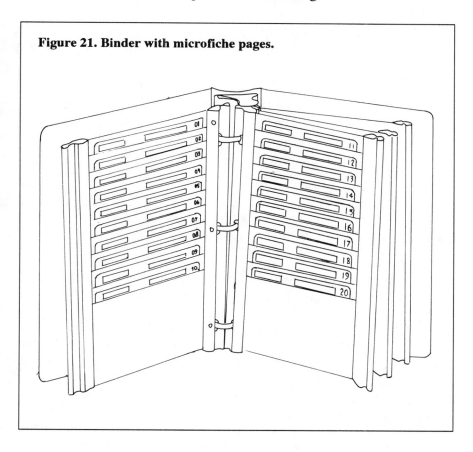

Figure 21. Binder with microfiche pages.

Figure 22. Book-like containers for microfiche and microcomputer discs.

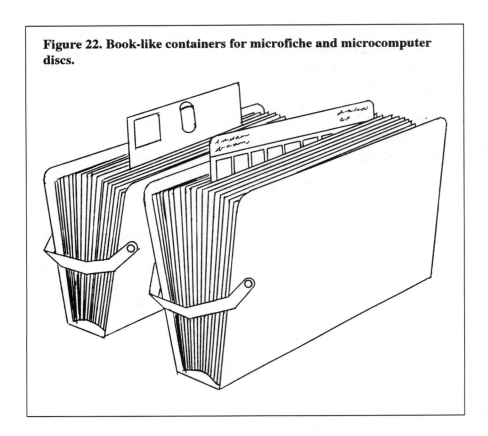

Partial Intershelving of Microforms

Hanging Devices. These devices, described in Chapter 4, can accommodate all formats of microforms (see Figure 9).

Trays. The trays described above may also be used for partial intershelving when there is a sufficient number of fiches, opaques, and cards in a classification range to make the trays an efficient use of space. In this case, specific classification numbers may be indicated on dividers made of inert material and the classification range of a tray's contents shown on an external label (see Figure 23).

Separate Media Shelves. Microfilms can be housed easily on the media shelves described in Chapter 4 (see Figure 4b).

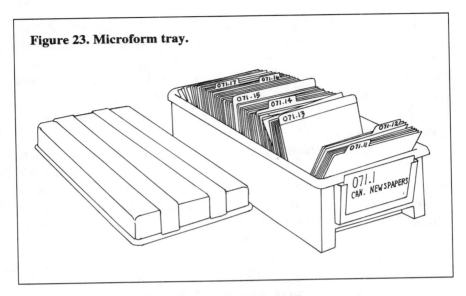

Figure 23. Microform tray.

Motion Pictures

Care and Handling

Motion picture collections in libraries are in decline due to the home VCR. Few patrons had their own motion picture projectors, particularly for 16-mm film, and the privilege of borrowing films usually meant a session of training and the transportation of equipment. How much more convenient it is to borrow a videocassette! Nevertheless, many libraries still have motion picture collections because some titles are only available in this format, and VCRs are not suitable for large group viewing, e.g., school classes.

Motion pictures are no longer marketed in cartridges or cassettes, although some are still used by firms for in-house systems. Cassettes and cartridges are included in this chapter for those libraries that still circulate them. Cartridges and cassettes are usually packaged in a manner suitable for intershelving. Because they are designed for a layperson's use, they can tolerate normal library wear and tear.

Reels should never be filled to the point where the film is flush with the edge of the reel; the edge of the reel should extend a minimum of ½ to 1 inch beyond the film. Reels should be in good condition. Bent, broken, rusty, chipped, nicked, or scratched reels will likely damage film and should be discarded. Plastic reels are preferable to metal reels because direct contact with metal and acetate supports may cause deterioration, and metal is more likely to bend and/or have sharp edges. Do not use imperfect plastic reels that have a line left from their molds. To prolong the life of a motion picture used once a year or less often, it should be stored on a plastic core and transferred to a reel before use.

Reels should be lifted by the hub or the lower flange to prevent damage to the edges of the film.

Only people who have proven their familiarity with motion picture projection should be allowed to run the equipment. They must be made aware that the equipment is never to be left during projection or rewinding and that the projector is to be stopped immediately if there are signs of trouble. Some types of equipment malfunctioning, e.g., scratching, can be discovered by running a length of black leader.

A five-foot leader and tail will help lessen the problems associated with dust, abrasion, and handling. A leader and tail of different colors can also help distinguish the beginning from the end of a motion picture.

Some libraries ask borrowers to return motion pictures unwound to save time on inspection equipment. Many libraries check each returned film; a rewound film run through inspection equipment must be rewound again after inspection, while an unwound film can be inspected and rewound at the same time. In addition, rewinding in the library is likely to be accomplished more correctly; an even wind is particularly important in the preservation of motion pictures.

A motion picture that is more than 30 years old should be carefully examined for shrinkage before it is put on any kind of transport machine, and if shrinkage is detected, expert advice should be obtained.

Storage

Horizontal versus vertical storage for open reels is controversial. Horizontal storage distributes stress more evenly and reduces potential distortion problems, but stress can be exerted on the bottom reels if the stacks are more than six or eight reels high. However, horizontal storage is inconvenient for circulation, so many libraries store their reel-to-reel motion pictures vertically. Vertical storage of large films allows the whole weight to rest on the lower layers causing a distortion of the image. This is not a problem of major concern for motion pictures that circulate actively.

Since easy access and an active collection are the premises of this book, the discussion will be confined to vertical storage.

Plastic storage containers are preferred to metal ones because of the potential for deterioration mentioned above.

Motion pictures should be stored no closer than 6 inches from the floor to reduce the incidence of dust and damage.

Intershelving of Motion Pictures

Boxes and Pamphlet Boxes. Any motion picture either received in a box or placed in a box which can stand upright by itself can be intershelved (see Figures 1h and 8f).

There are boxes specially fitted for large motion picture reels, such as fast lock cases, which will hold the reel firmly. It is important that they be shelved in a manner that minimizes the possibility of falling over. This can be effected by the use of clip-on holders or wire bookends attached to the bottom of the upper shelf. Freestanding bookends are not advised because they can shift easily.

Because of their small size, motion picture loop cartridges may be pushed out of sight to the back of the shelf. These can be held at the front of the shelf by placing them in the clip-on holders or modular units described below. Cartridges can also be housed in boxes or pamphlet boxes.

Clip-on Holders. These holders solve two problems associated with motion picture storage. Shallow holders will house small size cartridges at the front of the shelf, and tall clip-ons will hold larger motion picture reels in an upright position (see Figures 1g, 8e, and 19e).

A general description of clip-on holders is found in Chapter 4.

Modular Units. Modular units with one open side for browsing are another method of holding motion picture loop cartridges at the front of the shelf (see Figure 6). Most of these modules can accommodate two cartridges and have an interlocking device for stacking if greater capacity is required.

A general description of modular units is found in Chapter 4.

Partial Intershelving of Motion Pictures

Multimedia Shelves with Commercial Racks or Vertical Slots. Motion pictures housed in film cans need individual support for vertical housing (see Figures 6f and 8f). This can be accomplished by placing racks at one end of a shelf or by building vertical slots. Movable racks and slots are advisable if the expansion and shifting of the collection is a possibility.

Separate Media Shelves. Cartridges and small 8-mm reels can be housed on the media shelves described in Chapter 4 (see Figures 4a & f).

Hanging Devices. Hanging bags can accommodate small reels and cartridges. However, the bags are not strong enough to store heavy film in metal containers (see Figure 9).

A general description of hanging devices is found in Chapter 4.

Cartmobiles. Large reels can be stored on cartmobiles fitted with racks designed to hold the reels (see Figure 10).

A general description of cartmobiles is found in Chapter 4.

Transparencies

Care and Handling

Transparencies do not require the same degree of attention to their care and handling as do filmstrips, motion pictures, and slides. The base on which the photographic image is placed is generally more durable, and the diazo dyes used on transparencies do not fade as easily as photographic dyes. In addition, the projection light is spread over a wider surface and is, therefore, less damaging.

One aspect that distinguishes transparencies from other film media is the ability to add and remove additional information easily. Additions are usually made with a water-soluble ink marker, and removal with a damp, but not overly wet, cloth. Repeated writing on and cleaning may damage transparencies. Where this is likely to occur, a clear acetate sheet should be attached to transparencies accompanied by instructions to users to write on and erase the clear sheet.

Scratches and dust will show on the projected image, so it is wise to avoid these by housing transparencies in protective envelopes or folders and wiping them with a slightly damp, lint-free cloth after every use. A protective envelope with a window will facilitate browsing and decrease the amount of handling which always has a potential for damage.

Mounts are useful because they protect edges and prevent warping. Unmounted sets should have a sheet of acid-free paper between transparencies to protect them and prevent them from sticking together.

Storage

If the transparency mount is not strong or if the transparency is unmounted, it will buckle when shelved vertically. A rigid piece of cardboard or other material inserted in the protective envelope or folder will give support. All materials touching the transparency should be acid-free.

Transparencies should be stored in the same manner described for other two-dimensional materials in Chapter 8. These include:

- Envelopes (see Figure 28b later in Chapter 8). Envelopes made of plastic materials facilitate browsing and decrease direct handling by allowing the contents to be viewed without removal from the envelope. However, plastic materials may generate static electricity, thereby attracting dust. On the other hand, some authorities warn that storage in manilla envelopes may promote scratching. A general description of envelopes is found in Chapter 4.

- Binders (see Figure 6c). Three-ring binder pages specially adapted for transparencies can be purchased or made by the staff. Mounted transparency sets are sometimes housed in album-type binders because of their weight and bulk.

- Boxes and pamphlet boxes (see Figure 28e later in Chapter 8)

- Multimedia shelf with movable spacing panels (see Figure 6g)

- Multimedia shelf with pull-out racks or bins (see Figure 7)

- Multimedia shelf with commercial rack (see Figure 8)

- Hanging devices (see Figure 9)

Further Reading

Ach, William K. "Lighting in Microtext Rooms." *Microform Review.* 14 (3) (Summer 1985): 171–73.

American Library Association. Resources and Technical Services Division. Reproduction of Library Materials Section and Resources Section. *Microforms in Libraries: A*

Manual for Evaluation and Management, edited by Francis Spreitzer. Chicago: ALA, 1985.

Included are concise recommendations for the care, handling, and storage of microforms, equipment maintenance and repair, and a discussion about the pros and cons of circulating microforms and equipment.

Association for Information and Image Management. *Care and Handling of Active Microform Files.* AIIM Technical Report, TR13. Silver Spring, MD: AIIM, 1988.

――――――――. *Microspots and Aging Blemishes.* Special Interest Package, 34. Silver Spring, MD: AIIM, 1987.

A collection of articles on the causes of these defects and possible methods for prevention.

Association for Library Collections and Technical Services. *Guidelines for Packaging and Shipping Microforms.* Chicago: ALCTS, 1989. Free.

These guidelines may be of interest to libraries that interloan microforms or circulate them by mail.

Beatty, La Monde F. *Filmstrips.* The Instructional Media Library, 4. Englewood Cliffs, NJ: Educational Technology, 1981.

Step-by-step, illustrated instructions for splicing filmstrips are found on pages 75–79.

The Book of Film Care. Rochester, NY: Eastman Kodak, 1983.

An easy-to-read, illustrated discussion about the care, handling, and storage of motion pictures.

Boss, Richard W., with Raikes, Deborah. *Developing Microform Reading Facilities.* Microform Review Series in Library Micrographics Management, 7. Westport, CT: Microform Review, [19--].

Practical, readable, and well-illustrated discussions about the care and storage of microfilm, microfiche, ultrafiche, and microopaques.

Bowling, Mary B. "The Earl I. Sponable Papers: A Case History." *Conservation Administration News.* 20 (January 1985): 7–8, 26.

Film is included in this description of conservation methods applied to a collection received in bad condition.

Conway, Paul. "IPI Reports New Microfilm Permanence Research." *ACA Bulletin.* 13 (2) (November 1988): 13–14.

"Research scientists . . . have developed an improved image oxidation test to detect the potential for redox ('red spot') blemishing. They are now looking for ways to prevent such damage."

Dodson, Suzanne Cates. "Microfilm Types: There Really is a Choice." *Library Resources & Technical Services.* 30 (1) (January/March 1986): 84–90.

The author disputes the views of those who advocate diazo or vesicular film for long-term preservation.

――――――――. "Microfilm—Which Film Type, Which Application?" *Microform Review.* 14 (2) (Spring 1985): 87–94, 96–98.

Dupont, Jerry. "Microform Film Stock: A Hobson's Choice: Are Librarians Getting the Worst of Both Worlds?" *Library Resources & Technical Services.* 30 (1) (January/March 1986): 79–83.

An apologia for the use of diazo film for long-term preservation.

Fenstermann, Duane W. "Recommendations for the Preservation of Photographic Slides." *Conservation Administration News.* 31 (October 1987): 7.

A brief list of recommendations in point form about the care and handling of slides.

Green, Lee. *501 Ways to Use the Overhead Projector.* Littleton, CO: Libraries Unlimited, 1982.

Includes descriptions of different types of transparencies and suggestions for mounted and unmounted storage.

Hall, Hal W., and Michaels, George H. "Microform Reader Maintenance." *Microform Review.* 14 (1) (Winter 1985): 24–34.

A readable description of machine cleaning, troubleshooting, minor repairs, needed supplies, and tools.

Hendriks, Klaus B. *The Preservation and Restoration of Photographic Materials in Archives: A RAMP Study with Guidelines.* Paris: UNESCO, 1984.

A summary of "the currently available knowledge on the preservation and restoration of photographic materials" that, while including colored materials, emphasizes black-and-white materials; 185 citations in the bibliography.

Horder, Alan. *Guidelines for the Care and Preservation of Microforms in Tropical Countries,* prepared for the General Information Programme and UNISIST. Paris: UNESCO, 1990.

Irvine, Betty Jo, with the assistance of Fry, P. Eileen. *Slide Libraries: A Guide for Academic Institutions, Museums, and Special Collections.* 2nd ed. Littleton, CO: Libraries Unlimited, 1979.

Includes a discussion of different types of storage methods, a survey of works about environmental controls, and a detailed description of mounts.

Jones, Craig. *16 mm Motion Picture Film Maintenance Manual.* Consortium of University Film Centers Monograph Series, 1. Dubuque, IA: Kendall/Hunt, 1983.

A well-illustrated, detailed description of film damage, repair, and damage prevention, together with an overall view of storage.

Keefe, Lawrence E., Jr., and Inch, Dennis. *The Life of a Photograph: Archival Processing, Matting, Framing, and Storage.* Boston: Focal Press, 1984.

Included in this illustrated book are descriptions of adhesives, mounting, and various types of enclosures for photographs. One comprehensive chapter is devoted to the care, handling, and storage of color slides.

Laughlin, Mildred Knight, and Coty, Patricia Ann. "Overhead Transparencies". In *Nonbook Media: Collection Management and User Services,* edited by John W. Ellison and Patricia Ann Coty, pp. 214–26. Chicago: American Library Association, 1987.

McDonald, Peter. "Color Microform: New Possibilities." *Microform Review.* 17 (3) (August 1988): 146–49.

A description of types of color film, problems of fading, advantages and disadvantages of color microforms, and their cost effectiveness.

"Microfiche Curl." *Microform Review.* 16 (3) (Summer 1987): 228–30. Reprinted from *Innovator.* (July 1986).

A description of types of curl and suggestions for dealing with the problem.

Microfilm and Microfiche. Andover, MA: Northeast Document Conservation Center, 1987. Typescript. Available free from University Products, Holyoke MA.

Includes a description of film types, environmental conditions, care, and archival storage.

Patrie, Milton I. "How to Prevent Microfilm from Deteriorating." *Tech Trends* 30 (7) (October 1985): 28–29.

A brief, informal article on environmental conditions, helping patrons use equipment properly, and film cleaning, repair, and storage.

"Photogard." *Abbey Newsletter.* 10 (3) (October 1986): 70.

Describes "a process for coating film to protect it against heavy use."

Reilly, James M., et al. "Stability of Black-and-White Photographic Images, with Special Reference to Microfilm." *Abbey Newsletter.* 12 (5) (July 1988): 83–88. Reprinted in

Microform Review. 17 (5) (December 1988): 270–77.
A history of, and current research about, the problem of image oxidation.

Saffady, William. *Micrographics.* 2nd ed. Library Science Text Series. Littleton, CO: Libraries Unlimited, 1985.
A description of storage containers is found on pages 216–20.

Shontz, Marilyn L. "Microforms." In *Nonbook Media: Collection Management and User Services,* edited by John W. Ellison and Patricia Ann Coty, pp. 140–60. Chicago: American Library Association, 1987.

Spirt, Diana L. "Filmstrips." In *Nonbook Media: Collection Management and User Services,* edited by John W. Ellison and Patricia Ann Coty, pp. 69–84. Chicago: American Library Association, 1987.

Turner, Jeffrey H. "The Suitability of Diazo Film for Long Term Storage." *Microform Review.* 17 (3) (August 1988): 142–45.
A manufacturer's representative argues that "when used in an active file, diazo is likely to last as long, if not longer, than silver film."

Walker, Leslie J. "Slides." In *Nonbook Media: Collection Management and User Services,* edited by John W. Ellison and Patricia Ann Coty, pp. 338–48. Chicago: American Library Association, 1987.

Wiener, Paul B. "Films." In *Nonbook Media: Collection Management and User Services,* edited by John W. Ellison and Patricia Ann Coty, pp. 32–68. Chicago: American Library Association, 1987.

The following unpublished drafts are available from the Preservation Office, National Library of Canada (395 Wellington Street, Ottawa, ON, K1A 0N4). Although these papers are directed to NLC staff, some of the contents are useful for the care, handling, and storage of microforms in all libraries.

Lehn, Anna, and Michaels, Jan. "Optimal Handling Procedures for Microforms. Draft, July 3, 1990."

————. "Optimal Storage Conditions for Master and Preservation Copies of Canadian Microforms. Draft, March 13, 1989."

Chapter 8
Two-Dimensional Opaque Materials (Art Reproductions, Charts, Maps, Pictures, Postcards, Posters, Study Prints, Technical Drawings)

The conservation and preservation of paper-based materials has been a problem for libraries for many years. The manufacture of paper from wood products has resulted in paper that "self-destructs" over time. Research and archival libraries have become involved in deacidification projects, an expensive solution beyond the means of any but the largest libraries. "Permanent paper," which can be stored for long periods without discoloration or change in texture, has been developed and is now used by some publishers for their hardcover books. The results of the Canadian Department of Supply and Services' "Report on the Runability of Alkaline Paperstocks within the National Printing Bureau" show that it is cheaper to produce books on permanent paper; therefore, in the future we can expect permanent paper to have a wide use in publishing. An additional benefit is that less pollution is produced by mills making permanent paper than by those making acidic paper. Unfortunately, it is expensive to convert mills; conversion will take place when the industry feels a significant pressure from consumers. Libraries can contribute to this process by printing their own publications on permanent paper and making suppliers aware that they prefer to purchase materials made of permanent paper. An infinity symbol is used by publishers to indicate permanent paper. The comments in this chapter are directed toward the present collection of paper-based materials in libraries, most of which are inherently destructible.

Many two-dimensional, opaque materials in circulating collections are relatively inexpensive or free, and some should be replaced frequently to keep information up-to-date. There may also be fragile or rare items of permanent importance that need extra measures to ensure their preservation. Because paper is damaged easily, the costs of conservation must be balanced against those of replacement or the possibility of replacement. The comments in this chapter about care and handling should be considered with this in mind.

Since postcards, posters, and technical drawings are found infrequently in multimedia collections, they are not mentioned specifically in this chapter. However, they have been added to the chapter's title because the considerations for care, handling, and storage outlined below apply to them as well as to other two-dimensional opaque materials.

Some libraries circulate original works of art. In many instances the items belong to the artist who has an agreement with the library about their care, handling, storage, and circulation. Therefore, this chapter does not deal with two-dimensional original works of art, nor does Chapter 9 deal with three-dimensional works of art. Information about original art collections may be found in the citations listed at the end of the General Bibliography.

Care and Handling

Acid-free Materials. Acid-free folders and acid-free interleaving sheets will help lessen the inherent destructibility of paper because acid migrates from more to less acidic paper. The interleaving sheets will also protect the surface of an item from the abrasion of friction when two or more items are housed in the same container.

Cleanliness. A soft rubber eraser can remove much surface soil.

Acrylic Sprays. Acrylic spray can be used to protect and strengthen a sheet of paper. It also allows the sheet to retain its flexibility, if this is desired, and is relatively inexpensive. A spray should be first tested on an inconspicuous corner of an item to determine its compatibility with the ink and paper. It is better to apply two or three thin coats rather than one thick coat.

Edging. Edging helps to prevent fraying and tearing. This inexpensive procedure can be done manually or, more easily and probably more neatly, with a simple-to-use, hand-operated machine that applies tape around the edges of a sheet of paper. One drawback to this method is that it covers edges only, leaving most of the item vulnerable to dust, dirt, fingerprints, etc.

Folding. If an item made of paper is received folded, a method of indicating the original manner of folding should be devised so that it will always be refolded in the same way. Folding against the folds already in the paper will weaken these areas.

If an item is to be folded for storage purposes, it is best to make a single fold with the grain of the paper. Particularly in maps the fold should be placed where it is least likely to affect important information because the fold area is subject to deterioration. All folds should be reinforced, especially at the intersection of the fold lines. Adhesive cloth strips, tissues that are applied with water-soluble adhesives, or solvent-activated adhesives should be placed on areas of strain. Pressure-sensitive tape should not be used because it will stain and damage paper.

Some librarians fold materials so that the title and other significant information is displayed, thus minimizing the possibility of unnecessary handling. Other librarians fold the content of an item to the inside in order to protect the surface from dust and dirt. Where concern about dust and dirt is paramount, folded items should be placed in their containers, envelopes, etc., with the fold at the opening to the container. This gives more protection against dust and dirt and also against the possibility of pulling on one corner of an item during removal from the container.

An alternative method of folding (Figure 24) is to dissect the item into appropriately sized pieces, mount these pieces on a pressboard file folder spaced to permit folding, and place the folded item into a pamphlet binder, an envelope, or other suitable container for storage. Pressboard file folders can be purchased or made by staff.

Mounting. Mounting also lengthens the active life of a picture or map. If a flexible mount is needed because of the method of storage, backings made of linen, pure rag paper, Wabasso cotton, or some other durable nonacidic material are recommended. If the storage method requires the item to stand upright, the mount should be rigid enough to support the item but not so rigid that it will crack if subjected to pressure. The mount should be large enough so that there is a margin to absorb the wear and tear of

Figure 24. Dissected map mounted on pressboard file folder.

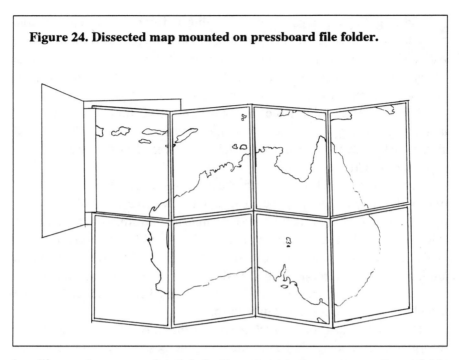

handling and accommodate labels. Expert mounting can smooth out folds and wrinkles and make previous repairs less conspicuous. However, if damage occurs after the item is mounted, repairs are more difficult. Mounting is not suitable for two-sided items because one side will be permanently lost. Dry mounting, though more expensive than wet mounting, is recommended for items that will be part of a permanent collection because wet mounting may hasten the deterioration process. Information on mounting methods and materials is found in Further Reading at the end of this chapter and in the General Bibliography.

An archival method (Figure 25) that can be used for single-sided materials is to mount an item on an acid-free board which is hinged to a second board. A window is cut in the top board and filled with a polyester film. This holds the item firmly and allows browsing, but it does not withstand active circulation as well as some other types of protection.

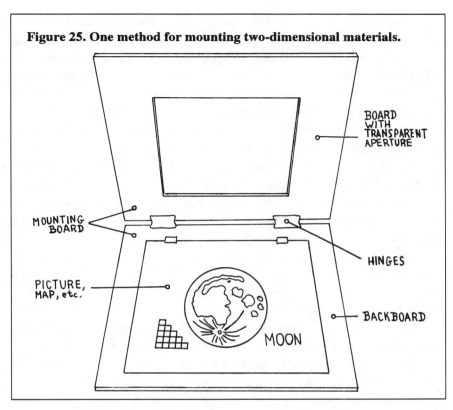

Figure 25. One method for mounting two-dimensional materials.

Lamination. Lamination protects and strengthens materials and will stand up well to the hazards of circulation. It allows both sides of an item to be viewed, which is not possible with mounted materials. Matte finish, which eliminates glare, is more expensive than gloss. Because seams in the laminate are subject to wear, it is important to buy laminate wide enough to cover an item. Large items should probably not be laminated because of the cost and the likelihood of seam wear.

There are two types of lamination:

(a) Cold lamination in which plastic film coated with a pressure-sensitive adhesive is applied manually to an item. Some firms sell "delayed-action" adhesive that does not set for 6–24 hours, allowing the contents of the enclosure to be adjusted after the initial application;

(b) Hot lamination in which the plastic film is bonded to an item by pressing together between hot plates or rollers. Many items must be laminated to justify the expense of a laminating machine.

Lamination will not prevent acidification; in fact, the heat of the press in hot lamination will speed up this process. If long-term use is anticipated, paper should be deacidified before lamination. However, the materials used in lamination will themselves eventually deteriorate, becoming brittle with age. Because of this and because an image may be permanently altered by fixing it to plastic, lamination is not appropriate for archival materials.

There is controversy about candidates for lamination. Since it is irreversible and will deteriorate in time, some librarians recommend it only for items that can be replaced easily or have limited value. Other librarians would use it only to add years of existence to items that cannot be treated by another method of conservation. Still others believe that hot lamination with its expensive equipment should be used for items with a high replacement cost and/or heavy use.

Encapsulation. Experts are agreed that encapsulation is preferred to mounting and lamination. In this method an item is placed between two sheets of polyester cut 2 inches wider than its outside dimensions and, after air has been forced out of the envelope, taped manually or with a machine that fuses or welds the edges of the film. Encapsulation does not require highly trained staff, is inexpensive if done manually, and is reversible.

Encapsulation will not prevent acidic materials from deteriorating. The Library of Congress, which has undertaken much research on encapsulation, recommends deacidification before encapsulation, but recognizes that deacidification is not possible for all libraries. Studies have revealed that encapsulation may hasten deterioration if the enclosure is tightly sealed. One or two sides of an enclosure must remain open to allow for the escape of gases and the movement of air. An alternate method is to enclose a carbonate-buffered paper with the encapsulated item.

> At the Library of Congress, undeacidified paper that was encapsulated together with a sheet of buffered paper behaved the same as if it had been deacidified.[1]

The Library of Congress also tested polyester and polypropylene as encapsulation materials. Shahani, Research Officer, Library of Congress reports:

> The rates of aging paper samples are identical inside polyester and polypropylene envelopes. Therefore, polypropylene film provides a viable and appreciably less expensive alternative to polyester film, especially for encapsulation of small items. . . . However, it lacks the

rigidity of polyester, and therefore cannot provide adequate support for larger items.[2]

Shrink Wrapping. This is a quick temporary method employed by some libraries for less valuable items. The item together with a stiff cardboard backing is enclosed in stretchable plastic film and sealed on the back with a hot iron. Some source of hot air (hair dryer, hot air gun) directed at the item tightens the film. Shrink wrapping does not give as effective a protection as encapsulation or lamination and should not be considered for valuable items or those expected to have long-term and/or heavy use. The advantages of shrink wrapping are that it is easily accomplished and easily reversed; the materials are cheaper; there is a less glimmering effect from reflected light.

Small holes should be made in the film to allow acidic gases to escape.

Storage

It is possible to purchase some pictures and maps in protective plastic formats, sometimes folded and with attached covers. These can be easily intershelved.

Two-dimensional opaque materials exist in a wide variety of sizes. Large items which cannot be conveniently folded to a size practical for shelving are discussed below under "Storage of Large Materials."

Intershelving of Two-Dimensional Opaque Materials

Envelopes. Many two-dimensional materials are an ideal size and shape for storage in the envelopes discussed in Chapter 4.

Inexpensive or ephemeral materials may not be worth the time and expense of careful conservation methods; they can be quickly and easily stored in plastic or manila envelopes and intershelved (see Figure 7b and later, in Chapter 9, Figure 35d). Large, brightly colored envelopes will prevent their being overlooked in the search for information. If the envelope used is not rigid enough for shelving, a piece of stiff cardboard should supply the necessary support. Alternately the item can be stapled to a brightly colored manila folder and intershelved. Both envelopes and folders can be housed in one of the methods described below for added protection.

Boxes and Pamphlet Boxes. Several items with the same classification number can be housed in a box, pamphlet box, or Princeton file (see Figures 34h and 35f later in Chapter 9). These items should have sufficient protection so that they will not be crushed or torn during browsing and circulation. The box can either be circulated as a unit or each item can be provided with the paraphernalia necessary for individual circulation.

A general discussion about boxes is found in Chapter 4.

Clip-on Holders. Two-dimensional materials, either individually or in envelopes, that need support to stand vertically can be housed in clip-on holders (see Figure 19e). These steel units with their colorful epoxy finishes also attract attention to thin materials which may otherwise be overlooked.

A general description of clip-on holders is found in Chapter 4.

Binders. Single items can be housed in pamphlet binders which are available in several sizes (see Figures 1m and 6c). If an item is smaller than an open pamphlet binder, it is folded in the middle and attached at this middle to the inner spine of the binder (see Figure 8d). An edge of a large single item can be attached to the inside of a pamphlet binder, and the item stored folded inside the binder in a manner that allows it to be unfolded easily to its fullest extent.

More protection for contents is furnished by the acid-free pamphlet binders marketed in several sizes with envelopes attached to their inner spines. These binders are also useful for items with loose pieces.

Ring and album binders are suited to sets of two-dimensional materials because they can hold a varying number of pieces and the contents can be viewed without direct handling. Plastic pages designed to hold two-dimensional materials, and laminated, mounted, and encapsulated items with ring holes punched in their margins, are stored in these binders and intershelved (see Figure 26). This method is limited to materials that are not larger than the binders.

A general description of binders is found in Chapter 4.

Partial Intershelving of Two-Dimensional Opaque Materials

Multimedia Shelf with Movable Spacing Panels. Items that can stand upright may be housed at the end of a shelf fitted with movable spacing panels (see Figure 6h). These can be placed wider apart than the measure-

Figure 26. Binder containing pictures.

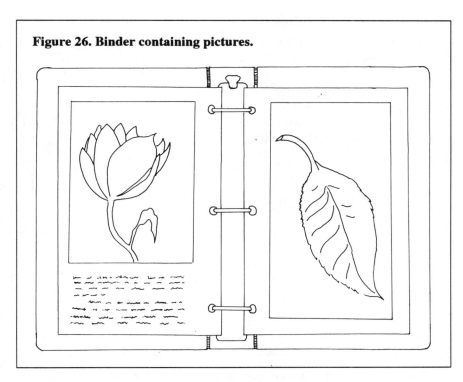

ment recommended for analog sound discs (see Chapter 5) because off-vertical stacking does not do the irreparable damage to two-dimensional opaque materials that it does to sound discs. If a library plans to house maps, pictures, transparencies, and sound discs together in vertical slots in a particular section of the collection, the panels should be 3½ to 4 inches apart.

Multimedia Shelf with Interlocking Units. Equipment designed for desk-top vertical files can also be used. Devices, such as "Add-A-File," can be expanded to house two-dimensional materials by adding interlocking units (see Figure 27).

Multimedia Shelf with Pull-Out Rack or Bin. This method is similar to that described for analog sound discs in Chapter 5. It is easier to browse the materials in the bin than in a rack; therefore, a bin is preferable because two-dimensional materials need not be held in the upright position required for sound discs. In order to utilize bins or racks, items must be the proper size, have some rigidity, or be in containers that provide support. A bin can be stationary if the position of the shelf allows its contents to be browsed easily (see Figure 28g).

Figure 27. Multimedia shelf with interlocking file units.

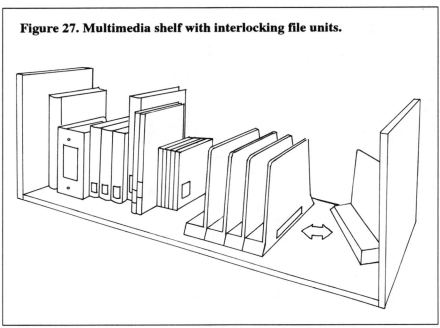

Figure 28. Multimedia shelf with stationary browser bin.

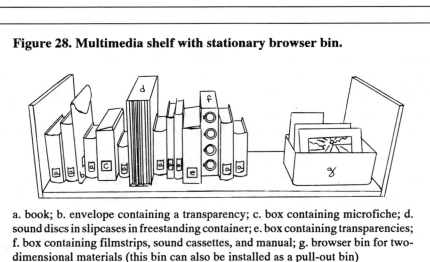

a. book; b. envelope containing a transparency; c. box containing microfiche; d. sound discs in slipcases in freestanding container; e. box containing transparencies; f. box containing filmstrips, sound cassettes, and manual; g. browser bin for two-dimensional materials (this bin can also be installed as a pull-out bin)

Multimedia Shelf with Commercial Rack. Another method described in Chapter 5 for shelving analog sound discs can be used to house fairly rigid two-dimensional materials of a suitable size (see Figure 8h).

Hanging Devices. Two-dimensional materials that can fit, or be folded to fit, into a hanging bag are well suited to this type of storage (see Figure 9). Many items may be browsed and circulated without removal from the bag.

A general description of hanging devices is found in Chapter 4.

Storage of Large Materials

A library with funding generous enough to provide much shelving space can intershelve all its materials, large and small, because it can devote one-third, one-half, or a whole shelf to one item. Most libraries are not as fortunate and must observe economy in shelving practice to a greater or lesser extent. In such cases, large size items must be housed elsewhere. However, a dummy should be placed in the classification sequence to indicate where the large item may be found, and the item should be stored as close as possible to the appropriate section of the collection.

Some large items may be awkward for borrowers to transport, particularly when patrons have not come to the library in cars. It is helpful if "carrying aids" can be provided when needed. The best carrying aids appear to be sturdy canvas bags. They are durable, light-weight, available commercially, relatively inexpensive, and accommodate different shapes and sizes. Several libraries report that handles on boxes eventually break, and the heavier the items transported, the sooner the break. Leather artists' cases are suitable for two-dimensional materials, but may not be a wise investment if a library plans to provide carrying aids for other heavy or awkwardly shaped materials because their rigid sides limit their flexibility.

Partial Intershelving of Large Two-Dimensional Materials

Rolled Storage. Experts disagree about whether rolled storage of large two-dimensional materials is advisable. Rolling and unrolling actively circulated items will undoubtedly cause deterioration. The seriousness of the deterioration is determined by the care exercised in handling. The following suggestions may help to alleviate some of the wear and tear.

- Items should always be rolled in the same direction and to the same diameter. If an item is received rolled, these factors should be noted.

- Items that have previously been folded should be rolled with the fold parallel, not perpendicular, to the roll.

- Items to be stored in a tube should be tied with a tape in a roll smaller in diameter than that of the tube, allowing the item to be removed easily without tearing or fraying. If for some reason it is difficult to remove the item, it is better to sacrifice the tube than to risk damaging its contents.

- Square boxes with dimensions similar to tubes make insertion and removal easier because the space left between the roll and the corners permits the contents to be grasped firmly. As with tubes, the items housed should be tied with tape in a roll smaller in diameter than the width of the box.

- Items may be wrapped around the outside of a tube and covered with a sheet of protective material, such as polyester or acid-free paper. This method avoids the potential problems associated with insertion in and removal from tubes.

- Rolled items are difficult to browse. They should be well labelled with enough information so that the need to roll and unroll is reduced. Because one end of a tube may be more visible at certain times than the other end, labels affixed to both ends may reduce the number of times a patron browsing the collection may need to shift the tubes to see descriptive information.

- The end of a tube or box that rests on a hard surface when stored upright can be subject to damage during placement in the storage device. The tube or box should extend one inch beyond its contents for added protection.

Rolls, and in many cases boxes, can be stored in umbrella stands, racks intended for wine bottles, bins, cardboard boxes with partitions, as well as in traditional devices (see Figures 29 and 30). Some libraries have attached uprights to the front of a shelf to prevent rolls from falling. Others have affixed back-sloping pegs to walls to hold rolls.

Mobile Study Print Bins, Art Print Units, and Poster Bins. Study prints are frequently produced on cardboard, which does not lend itself to folding or rolling. They are too large to be housed effectively on a standard shelf. These and other materials with similar dimensions can be stored in study print bins placed near the shelves with the appropriate classification. Mounted items that are too large for study print bins can be placed in poster bins or in art print shelving units.

Figure 29. Roll storage.

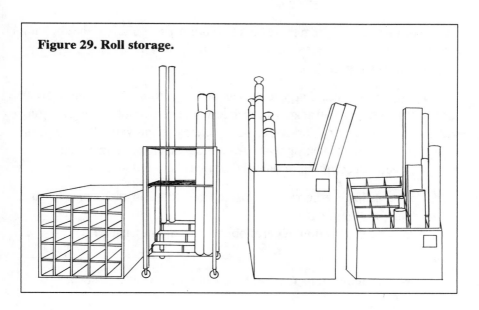

Figure 30. Roll storage.

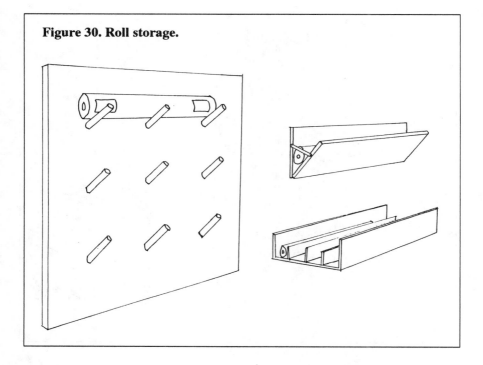

It is not necessary that these bins be mobile, particularly if the shelving of the collection tends to be static. Mobility is useful with a growing collection (see Figure 31).

Hanging Devices. Large items can be hung from a free-standing rack or one attached to a wall at an appropriate height. Especially strong hanging devices are necessary for large, heavy items to prevent damage from warpage, sagging, or tearing away from mounts, clips, hangers, etc.

A general description of hanging devices is found in Chapter 4.

Cartmobiles. Large rigid items can be stored in racks placed on a cartmobile (see Figure 10).

A general description of cartmobiles is found in Chapter 4.

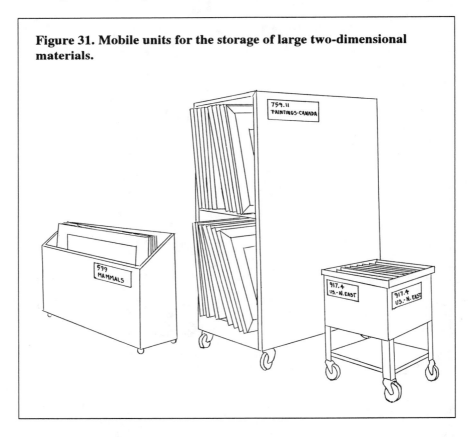

Figure 31. Mobile units for the storage of large two-dimensional materials.

References

1. "Encapsulation Research," *Abbey Newsletter,* vol. 10, no. 1 (February 1986): 1.
2. Chandru J. Shahani, "Letters," *Abbey Newsletter,* vol. 10, no. 2 (April 1986): 20.

Further Reading

Association for Library Service to Children. Print and Poster Evaluation Committee. *Developing and Managing a Print and Poster Collection for Children.* [Chicago]: ALCS, [19--]
Includes an overview of surface protection, mounting, framing, circulation procedures, display, and storage.

Coleman, J. Gordon, Jr. "Flat Pictures, Posters, Charts, and Study Prints." In *Nonbook Media: Collection Management and User Services,* edited by John W. Ellison and Patricia Ann Coty, pp. 85–93. Chicago: American Library Association, 1987.

Cunha, George M.; Lowell, Howard P.; and Schnare, Robert E. *Conservation Survey Manual.* [S.l.]: Section on the Management of Information Resources and Technology of the New York Library Association, 1982.
Descriptions of surface cleaning, paper repair with a recipe for paste, and polyester film encapsulation with illustrations are found on pages 31–40.

Cunningham, Veronica Colley. "The Preservation of Newspaper Clippings." *Special Libraries.* 78 (1) (Winter 1987): 41–46.
A discussion of climate control, care, handling, storage, preservation methods, and the advantages and disadvantages of microfilming over keeping a newspaper in its original form.

Ehrenberg, Ralph E. *Archives & Manuscripts: Maps and Architectural Drawings.* SMA Basic Manual Series. Chicago: Society of American Archivists, 1982.
Pages 42–52 deal with archival storage and conservation including flattening, surface cleaning, mending, reinforcement, neutralization and buffering, polyester film encapsulation, matting, and framing.

Encapsulation. Andover, MA: Northeast Document Conservation Center, 1987. Typescript. Available free from University Products, Holyoke, MA.
Illustrated, step-by-step instructions.

Farrell, Barbara, and Debarats, Aileen. *Guide for a Small Map Collection.* 2nd ed. Ottawa: Association of Canadian Map Libraries, 1984.
Includes the care, handling, and storage of maps in a single medium collection.

Greenfield, Jane. *Books, Their Care and Repair.* New York: H.W. Wilson, 1983.
Included in this well-illustrated book are discussions about the causes of paper deterioration, paper treatment, encapsulation, adhesives, mending, pamphlet binders, and a list of suppliers.

Gunner, Jean. *Simple Repair and Preservation Techniques for Collection Curators, Librarians and Archivists.* 2nd ed. Pittsburgh, PA: Hunt Institute for Botanical Documentation, Carnegie-Mellon University, 1984.
This well-illustrated book includes encapsulation, matting, and the construction of boxes.

Herring, Billie Grace. "Art Reproductions." In *Nonbook Media: Collection Management and User Services,* edited by John W. Ellison and Patricia Ann Coty, pp. 1–19. Chicago: American Library Association, 1987.

Larsgaard, Mary Lynette. *Map Librarianship: An Introduction.* 2nd ed. Littleton, CO: Libraries Unlimited, 1987.

Pages 163–97 include a practical, easy-to-read discussion about environmental problems, handling, care, repair, and storage with reference to other sources. Brief mention of globes and microforms. Lists of publishers and suppliers are found in the appendices.

Library of Congress. Preservation Office. *Paper and Its Preservation: Environmental Controls.* Rev. ed. Preservation Leaflet, 2. Washington, DC: Library of Congress, 1983. Free.

Includes the composition of paper, causes of deterioration, the effect of temperature and humidity, pollutants, light, mold, insects and rodents, and a brief list of suppliers.

Library of Congress. Preservation Office Research Services. *Polyester Film Encapsulation.* LC Publications on Conservation of Library Materials. Washington, DC: Library of Congress, 1980.

Provides step-by-step illustrated instructions for making a basic polyester envelope.

McCrady, Ellen. "Accelerated Aging and the Effects of Enclosure." *Abbey Newsletter.* 8 (2) (April 1984): 28–29.

A discussion of the effect on contents of encapsulation and shrink wrapping.

Melton, L.J. "Oblong Posters in Round Tubes." *Unabashed Librarian.* 18 (Winter 1976): 26.

A public librarian describes a cheap storage unit for posters made from tennis ball tubes donated by local tennis clubs.

Minter, William. "Polyester Encapsulation Using an Ultrasonic Welding Machine." Paper delivered at the 1985 IFLA Conference Joint Meeting of Conservation and Science and Technology. Typescript.

A description of a new technique for sealing the edges of polyester film.

National Library of Canada. Program for Canadian Newspapers. Working Group on Original Issues of Canadian Newspapers. *Guidelines for the Treatment of Canadian Newspapers in Original Newsprint Form.* 1988. Typescript. Free.

This bilingual report includes recommendations that can be applied to all paper materials.

Nichols, Harold. *Map Librarianship.* 2nd ed. London: Bingley, 1982.

The chapter on storage discusses horizontal, vertical, roll, and display shelving including comments on intershelving, and ends with a list of British manufacturers of map and plan storage equipment.

"Permanent Paper: Questions and Answers." *National Library News.* 22 (3–4) (March–April 1990): 6–7. (Also available as a pamphlet in English and French. Free.)

Outlines the advantages of permanent paper and urges libraries to support its use in their own libraries and by publishers.

Rieke, Judith. "Keepers of Maps: Some Advice on Preservation." *Wilson Library Bulletin.* 60 (2) (October 1985): 25–27.

A discussion about storage in drawers and vertical cases, circulation, preservation by edging, lamination, and encapsulation, and repair of mechanical damage.

Rieke, Judith L.; Gyeszly, Suzanne; and Steele, Leslie. "Preservation of Sheet Maps, Lamination or Encapsulation: A Durability Study." *Special Libraries Association Geography and Map Division Bulletin.* 138 (December 1984): 2–10.

A cost analysis and study of the effectiveness of lamination and encapsulation for the preservation of heavily used maps.

Ross, Leslie. "Picture Files: An Important Resource." *BCLA Reporter.* 29 (1) (January 1985): 12–13.

A very brief overview of acquisitions, cataloging, and storage.

"Self Preservation: Quick Display Protection for the Intrepid Map Librarian." *Western Association of Map Libraries Information Bulletin.* 18 (1) (November 1986): 66–68. Describes shrink wrapping as an alternative to encapsulation, followed by a study of the effect of encapsulation on paper documents. Includes sources of supply.

Woodson, Ernest L. "Maps." In *Nonbook Media: Collection Management and User Services,* edited by John W. Ellison and Patricia Ann Coty, pp. 128–39. Chicago: American Library Association, 1987.

Chapter 9
Three-Dimensional and Boxed Materials (Dioramas, Games, Globes, Kits, Models, Realia)

Because of the great diversity in size, shape, and materials used in the manufacture of three-dimensional and many-piece boxed materials, this chapter will provide only very general directions for their care and handling.

The size and awkward shape of some items should not discourage their storage on open shelving because three-dimensional materials usually draw attention and create interest in their subject matter. They may also attract potential patrons.

Care and Handling

Cleanliness. Dust can be reduced by placing transparent dust covers over models, dioramas, and globes when not in use. Other items can be stored in plastic bags which are then placed in a container. Three-dimensional materials should be dusted from time to time and wiped with a damp cloth to remove dirt. Some materials can be washed with warm, soapy water. It is preferable to use pure soap or detergents especially manufactured for museum use.

If an item is likely to attract insects, it should be sprayed once a year with an insect spray or powder.

Surface Protection. Items that have painted or paper-covered surfaces can be coated with a clear polyurethane varnish. This will add protection and help the items to retain a "brand new" appearance. Other items, e.g., certain kinds of realia, can be protected by spraying them lightly with some forms of plastic.

Items with Many Parts. Boxed materials consisting of many parts can present an irritating problem. It seems inevitable that some parts will be lost and others placed in the wrong box. In a circulating collection this problem will never be completely solved. But it can be minimized. An inventory of the contents and/or a photograph of the parts of an item (see page 17 for a description of the use of such photographs taken during the cataloging process) should be attached to the lid with a note asking the patron to check the contents before and after use and to report any missing part. This will help to make a patron aware of the need to keep track of the parts.

If pieces fit snugly into a container, and once removed are difficult to repack, a picture of the proper arrangement attached to the container may prevent damage from the forcing of parts.

If it is feasible, all parts, including a dust cover, should be labelled. Unique call numbers may give sufficient identification.

Removable parts can be tied onto a basic model or globe or to a dust cover. If possible, the parts should be tied in such a way that the patron does not have to untie the parts in order to use the item.

Instructions can be copied when an item is received and spare copies kept filed by call number in a spare copy box in the workroom. Instructions on a single-sided sheet can be attached permanently to the container. One of the protective coverings described in Chapter 8 can be used to lengthen the life of an instruction sheet.

Fragile Materials. Some items of realia may be fragile. These should be mounted, displayed, or preserved in ways that will not destroy their usefulness. For example, a container housing seed samples must be moisture free. Delicate realia should not be able to move in the container. Padding can be added or a vial the exact size of the specimen selected as a container. A cicada picked up from a cottage floor and placed without preservatives in a transparent vial that fitted its dimensions survived intact the careless handling of the vial by 150 cataloging students, while a plastic skeleton commercially packaged in flimsy celluloid crumbled to pieces after being examined by 25 students.

Some experts advocate storage in light-tight containers because of the deteriorating effect light has on some items. Certain bottles and other containers used by the drug industry have been specially treated to block damaging rays. A Royal Ontario Museum staff member recommends the use of old-fashioned colored cellophane because it breathes and filters out some of the harmful light rays. The noise created when it is touched acts as a signal to an item's delicate nature. However, items in light-filtering containers cannot be viewed without removing them from the containers. The potential damage from light will have to be balanced against that from handling before a decision is made concerning transparent or light-filtering packaging for each item. My experience with many pieces of realia leads to the conclusion that proper packaging is a much more important preservation measure than protection against artificial light. The reason the cataloging class's cicada has remained intact for a number of years is that it is never removed from the vial, and there is no possibility of movement within it. It has never been exposed to sunlight; however, there appears to be no visible deterioration from many periods of 2 to 3 months in fluorescent classroom lighting.

Storage

There is more challenge in the effective shelving of three-dimensional materials than of any other type of material. There are fewer commercial products available to aid in their shelving, and very little has been written on the subject. Storage devices should be durable; allow accessibility; facilitate, or at a minimum not hinder, transportation of items; and have space for adequate labelling.

Intershelving of Three-Dimensional and Boxed Materials

Boxes and Box-like Containers. Many items are sold in boxes designed for shelving. For example, some producers advertise "bookcase boxed games." Other manufacturers pare costs by using flimsy boxes. Some kits are marketed in boxes that are too large in relation to their contents. These waste space and/or overhang shelving. Suitable boxes may have to be made by library staff or volunteers for large and/or awkwardly shaped items.

A many-piece item can be a mystifying jumble in a box. Isolating similar components may add to an item's usefulness. This can be accomplished by placing similar components in plastic bags, by constructing compartments in containers, or by buying boxes with compartments (see Figures 1, 7f, 8b, 28f, 32a, and 34).

A general discussion about boxes and possible solutions to these problems is found in Chapter 4.

Figure 32. Transparent containers.

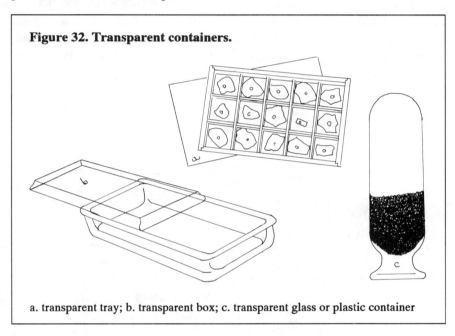

a. transparent tray; b. transparent box; c. transparent glass or plastic container

Trays. Transparent plastic trays and similar containers, with and without lids, are commercially available, particularly from scientific suppliers (see Figure 32b). These are useful in housing small objects, e.g., a collection of minerals, the pieces of a reading readiness skill game, a model. Very small pieces should be kept in a plastic bag in the tray to minimize the chance of the loss of a part. Trays are easily intershelved.

Unusually Shaped Containers. Containers with unusual shapes help to call attention to their contents (see Figure 32c).

Clip-on Holders. A poorly packaged kit of two or three items can be housed in a clip-on holder (see Figure 7g). These units are sold in a variety of designs to accommodate filmstrips and/or sound tapes and/or shelf-size two-dimensional materials and/or microfilms and manuals. Because these items are not housed in a container that will be circulated, they should be well labelled so that they can be reshelved easily.

A general description of clip-on holders is found in Chapter 4.

Modular Shelving Units. If a section of the classification contains many large three-dimensional and boxed items, it may be helpful to purchase modular shelving units with movable shelves which can accommodate unusual shapes (see Figure 33). Some manufacturers market such shelving in lightweight, durable materials which can be shifted without back strain. An amateur carpenter on the staff may also provide innovative modules designed for the specific materials to be shelved.

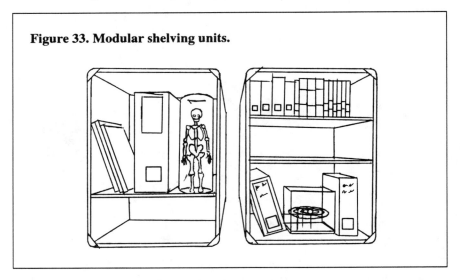

Figure 33. Modular shelving units.

Partial Intershelving of Three-Dimensional and Boxed Materials

Multimedia Shelf with Storage Compartments. Small items in trays, bags, or other transparent containers can be housed in a storage compartment placed on one end of a shelf. These compartments are marketed by scientific supply companies as "storage centers" or "display cases." They are enclosed on all sides except for an open side facing the public and are divided into a number of cubicles which can house small containers (see Figure 34).

Figure 34. Multimedia shelf with storage for small items.

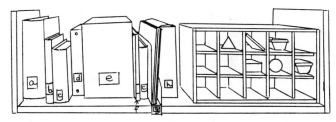

a. book-like album containing filmstrip set and manual; b. book-like album containing microcomputer cassettes; c. book; d. binder containing microcomputer disks; e. model in box; f. pamphlet binder containing a microfiche page; g. sound discs in slipcases in clip-on holder; h. box containing a set of maps

Multimedia Shelf with Rack. Boxed materials of a suitable size can be placed in racks which sit on one end of a shelf (see Figure 8). The boxes should not be so large that they overhang the shelf by an appreciable amount, because the boxes can be damaged or the boxes and/or the other contents of the shelf thrown to the floor by a staff member or patron inadvertently hitting the overhang while passing the shelf.

Separate Media Shelf. Small boxed items can be stored on the media shelves described in Chapter 4 (see Figure 4g, h, & i).

Items kept in plastic bags or small, ephemeral items that do not warrant conservation measures can be housed in labelled trays stored on a series of separate shelves built in the space of a regular shelf (see Figure 35). This series of shelves makes an efficient use of space, because the shelves can be spaced just enough to accommodate the trays.

Hanging Devices. Hanging bags (discussed in Chapter 4) can accommodate many shapes, but they are limited in the size and weight of the items that can be housed in them (see Figure 9).

Partial Intershelving of Large Size or Awkwardly Shaped Three-Dimensional and Boxed Materials

Cartmobiles. Large and awkwardly shaped items can be housed on cartmobiles with flat shelves or those with racks (see Figures 10 and 36). A general description of cartmobiles is found in Chapter 4.

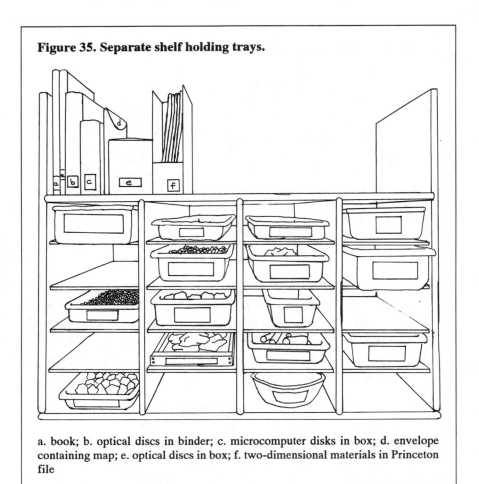

Figure 35. Separate shelf holding trays.

a. book; b. optical discs in binder; c. microcomputer disks in box; d. envelope containing map; e. optical discs in box; f. two-dimensional materials in Princeton file

Tables or Stands. An alternative to the expense of cartmobiles is to substitute a suitably sized table or stand that is not needed elsewhere. These should be placed as close to the appropriate section of the classification as possible.

Upper and Lower Shelves. Large and/or awkwardly shaped items can be placed on top shelves and stools/steps provided for patron and staff use where removal from these shelves might be clumsy or difficult. Very long items can be placed on any shelf where shelving units are placed back-to-back and intervening partitions removed.

Even though placement on less accessible shelves does not encourage, or in some cases permit, browsing, the size and general bright coloring of the items will attract the patrons' notice. In addition, a dummy placed in the appropriate classification sequence will also alert patrons to their existence. While not ideal, this shelving is better than having media housed unseen in the workroom.

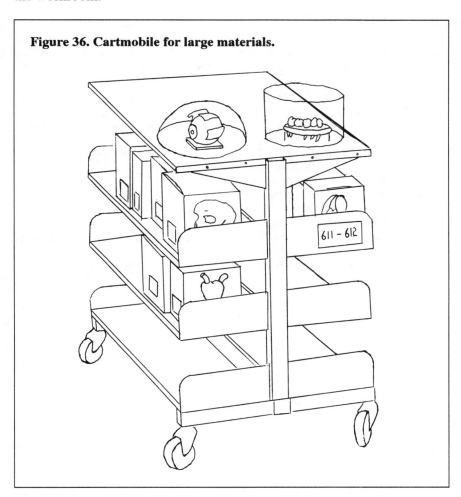

Figure 36. Cartmobile for large materials.

Imaginative Shelving Ideas

A Toronto library stores items in steamer trunks, suitcases, briefcases, flight bags, refrigerator dishes, dishpans, clothes hampers, etc. The container is usually related to the contents, e.g., a wicker beach basket holds seashells and a pamphlet on life in the oceans. This packaging adds interest to the subject for the patrons and can be fun for the library staff who think up an appropriate container and then look for it at secondhand stores and rummage sales. This type of packaging does not require much money, only ingenuity and the right staff chemistry.

Further Reading

Bierbaum, Esther Green. "Realia." In *Nonbook Media: Collection Management and User Services*, edited by John W. Ellison and Patricia Ann Coty, pp. 297–323. Chicago: American Library Association, 1987.

Hektoen, Faith H., and Rinehart, Jeanne R., eds. *Toys to Go: A Guide to the Use of Realia in Public Libraries*. Chicago: American Library Association, 1976.
Includes circulation procedures and a chart on the advantages and disadvantages of various containers and devices.

Soulier, J. Steven. *Real Objects and Models*. The Instructional Media Library, 12. Englewood Cliffs, NJ: Educational Technology, 1981.
There is a brief discussion of care and handling on pages 63–67.

Tessmer, Kathleen M. "Models." In *Nonbook Media: Collection Management and User Services*, edited by John W. Ellison and Patricia Ann Coty, pp. 161–80. Chicago: American Library Association, 1987.

Toy Libraries: How to Start a Toy Library in Your Community. Toronto: Canadian Association of Toy Libraries, 1978.
This pamphlet includes brief suggestions for care, circulation, and repair, and instructions for making toy bags.

Chapter 10
Microcomputer Disks

During the 1980s microcomputer disks, frequently called floppy disks or diskettes, gradually took their place in many library collections. Even libraries that do not include these disks in their collection policies find they sometimes accompany a book purchase or are part of a kit. Many libraries are now reporting several years of successful circulation and, as computers become a part of everyday life for many people, library collections of computer software may be expected to increase.

Computer science is a rapidly developing field. Applications, equipment, and associated software become outdated in a few years time; new products sometimes do not gain public acceptance and are discarded. This chapter concentrates on the most commonly used disks at the beginning of the 1990 decade: the 5¼-inch disk (also called a minifloppy diskette) and the 3½-inch disk (also called a microfloppy diskette). However, much of the content also applies to older types of disks, such as the 8-inch disk, or to new types on the market that do not yet have wide use, such as the 2-inch disk.

Library circulation of microcomputer disks is implicit in this discussion of their care, handling, and storage. It is assumed, therefore, that a library has resolved any copyright problems.

Care and Handling

A primary objective of all care, handling, and storage procedures is to protect a microcomputer disk against loss of data inscribed on it. Loss of part of the data is more serious in this medium than it is in other media. For example, damage to a sound tape may cause a few bars of music to be lost where the tape has been spliced, annoying but not disastrous. On the other hand, the loss of data in a disk's directory may result in an inability to call up files even though there has been no damage to the files themselves. Just one affected bit may cause chaos.

While the 3½-inch disk in its rigid plastic shell is more durable than the 5¼-inch disk in its flexible jacket, it is not indestructible. It should be handled with care even though it does not require the same degree of protection as the 5¼-inch disk.

Protection of Stored Data. The data on a disk can be destroyed even though the carrier of that data, the disk itself, is not damaged. The first action to be taken when a disk arrives in the library is to cover the write-protect notch on the 5¼-inch disk with an appropriate adhesive tab. These tabs are found in boxes of blank disks or can be purchased from a computer supply organization. A 3½-inch disk should be examined to ensure that the shutter on the write-protect notch is in the correct position. Covering these notches will protect the disk from accidental erasure or unwanted additions.

The second action is to make a copy of the disk, if this is possible. (Some disks are copy protected.) Unlike some other media, there is no quality difference between an original disk and its copy. Either one can be used for circulation. The one not processed for circulation should be kept in a fire-proof, dust-resistant container. This back-up disk will only be used to make another copy if the circulation copy is damaged or has been in use for some time. Disks lose their read/write capability over time; the newer disks have a much longer reliable span than older disks. It may be preferable to keep copies on tape or on write-once-read-many (WORM) compact disc formats which have longer-term stability.

Most software programs need detailed instructions for their operation. These instructions, frequently called documentation, are easily lost, misplaced, or damaged resulting in either an inability to use a program or to use it effectively. Any materials accompanying disks that instruct users in the operation of a program or in the manipulation of data should be duplicated, if possible. (Some copyright agreements specifically forbid the duplication of accompanying materials.) The original should be kept in a staff work area and used only to produce more copies. Some programs have substantial manuals in paperback or looseleaf format. These manuals should be treated with the same preservation methods as the book collection to lessen the likelihood of deterioration from broken spines, torn looseleaf holes, etc. On the other hand, if manuals are subject to frequent updates, their preservation may not be a worthwhile investment. Libraries should develop a policy about updates and the steps to be taken for their care.

Microcomputer disks are magnetic media and are subject to the same hazards from magnetic fields as magnetic tape (see Chapter 6). Disks should not rest on top of external disk drives. It has been suggested that paper clips recently held in a magnetic dispenser should not be allowed closer than three inches from a disk. Never rest a telephone on top of a disk drive or a container housing disks. A ringing telephone may erase data. However, library security systems should not be a problem. Most electronic detection systems and magnetic security systems with weak magnetic fields will not erase disks, but it is best to check with the manufacturer of the system to be certain.

Protection of the Physical Disk. Cleanliness is extremely important. Any deposits, such as dust, cigarette smoke, hair, fingerprints, can affect the stored electronic charge. Five-and-one-quarter-inch disks should always be kept in their paper envelopes when not in use and housed in covered containers. Fingers should be kept away from access holes on a disk's flexible jacket/plastic shell and disks should be handled by their labels.

Write on a label before affixing it to a 5¼-inch disk. If a disk is marketed with a label, use a felt tip pen rather than implements that require pressure, such as ball-point pens. Pencils are to be avoided not only because pressure is applied in writing and graphite may produce particulate matter, but also because graphite can become electrostatically charged. These caveats do not apply to the 3½-inch disk; any type of pen or pencil can be used on its shell. Be careful not to cover any holes in a disk jacket/shell with a label and, of course, objects should never be inserted in any openings.

Specialists advocate that liquids or sprays should not be used near disks because of the residue left when the moisture dries, and they recommend that any disk that has been in contact with liquids be discarded. However, damage from liquids may not have serious consequences for 5¼-inch disks. Kovacs discusses an experiment in which wet disks were made usable. Olson describes the successful salvaging of over 100 microcomputer disks thoroughly wetted by a burst pipe. Osborne cleaned disks contaminated with substances, ranging from a variety of liquids and food to hand cream, which may be found near computers and computer users.[1] Despite these successful experiences liquids and other contaminating matter should be kept away from disks.

The fumes from some substances can soften a disk coating. Avoid the use of solvents, nail polish, glue, cleaners, etc. in the vicinity of disks. Disks should never be cleaned.

In order to function properly a 5¼-inch disk must be able to spin smoothly in its flexible jacket. Care must be taken to ensure that it neither bends nor warps. Never use paper clips, even temporarily, on protective envelopes and certainly never on disks; paper clips can cause creases that create friction. To prevent warpage disks should be kept away from direct sunlight, sources of heat, and areas of high humidity.

Disks should be inserted carefully without force into a disk drive. Pressure can cause damage to the disk drive and 5¼-inch disks to bend.

Libraries discourage the use of book drops for the return of microcomputer disks. However, Polly reports that despite the library's pleas, many disks have been returned in the book drop and suffered no damage.[2]

Protection of the Computer. All computers should have surge protection from power surges caused by lightning, malfunctioning central power sources, etc.

Experts disagree about whether computers in use on any particular day should be turned on and off. Some people claim that turning computers off when not in use saves electricity and that with the rapid development of technology a computer will be outdated long before the on/off action causes damage. Other people recommend that computers be left on continuously because the small power surge when a computer is turned on will help to shorten its "hassle-free" life and may not be economic in the long run. As well, switches turned on and off frequently will wear out more quickly. Although there is differing opinion about turning on and off computers, there is general agreement that turning off monitors, particularly color monitors, when not in use is cost effective. Indeed, systems left on for an extended period will cause the image to be burned to some monitors.

There is also controversy about whether read/write heads should be cleaned, how often, and by what method.

Care should be taken when computers are moved to ensure that they are not jarred and that disks are removed from the disk drives. A strong bump can cause malfunctioning or the read/write head to fall on a disk.

Remove old labels before replacing them with new ones because extra layers of paper labels may catch in the disk drive.

Storage

Disks should be stored upright. Two or more disks housed in a container should not be packed too tightly because of the danger of "magnetic seep" from one disk to another. Pressure can also result in bending and distortion of a 5¼-inch disk's surface.

Most software sold by commercial organizations is marketed in boxes that contain both disks and accompanying documentation. These boxes are easily intershelved. Because of potential damage from paper dust, disks should not be housed in cardboard containers unless the disks are enclosed in a protective covering with a dust-resistant closure. However, since much of the software sold by medium-to-large commercial organizations has restrictive copyright agreements, libraries are more likely to circulate public domain software and shareware, which are not generally packaged in attractive, descriptive boxes. These items must be housed in containers acquired for this purpose. The many containers marketed for storing disks in offices, homes, and libraries do not provide storage for accompanying documentation. Since, in most instances, documentation is essential for the effective use of microcomputer programs and is too large to be enclosed in these containers, storage methods that do not allow disks and associated documentation to be housed together are not discussed in this chapter.

Some libraries place colored dots, indicating the required type of operating system, on the spine of a container as a guide to patrons and staff, thereby reducing the amount of unnecessary handling.

Intershelving of Microcomputer Disks

Boxes and Pamphlet Boxes. There are many storage boxes, sometimes called "cases" or "files," being marketed in a wide assortment of sizes and prices to house disks. Plastic boxes that hold one, two, or three disks give good protection and are easy to intershelve (see Figures 19f and 35c). In most instances these boxes are not a suitable storage medium by themselves because they cannot accommodate accompanying materials which must, therefore, be stored elsewhere. These boxes may, however, be used to protect disks when both disks and associated documentation are placed in general use boxes, pamphlet boxes, or Princeton files. It is important that 5¼-inch disks not be housed in general use boxes without rigid protection.

A general discussion about boxes is found in Chapter 4.

Book-like Albums. Albums similar to the ones developed for other media are available for microcomputer disks. They have compartments on one inside cover for one or two disks and on the opposite side for accompanying documentation. Only albums with dust-resistant closures or deep disk pockets should be used (see Figure 3).

A general description of book-like albums is found in Chapter 4.

Binders. Storage in binders is another method of housing disks and documentation together (see Figures 34d and 37). Binder pages for disks should be made of anti-static, nonabrasive materials that will not shed debris. Either the page pockets or the binders should have dust-resistant closures.

Manufacturers are marketing clear plastic holders with pressure-sensitive backings that accommodate disks in their paper envelopes. These holders protect disks from dust and dirt and can be affixed to pamphlet binders. Pamphlet binders provide support for disks and housing for accompanying documentation.

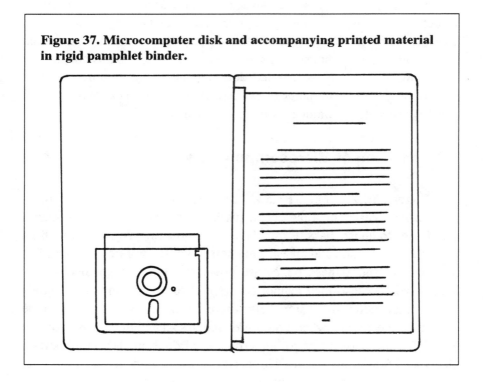

Figure 37. Microcomputer disk and accompanying printed material in rigid pamphlet binder.

Some pamphlet binders are marketed with "half pockets" into which disks can be inserted easily. These should be avoided because disks can fall out when the binder is not carried carefully.

A general description of binders is found in Chapter 4.

Book-like Containers. Each 3½- or 5¼-inch disk in its paper envelope may be inserted into a separate pocket of a book-like container (see Figure 22). The number of pockets can be varied according to the size of the set. The container should not be filled to the point that the disks are under pressure. This type of container is easily intershelved.

Clip-on Holders. Narrow clip-on holders will provide additional protection and support for disks and documentation where needed.

A general description of clip-on holders is found in Chapter 4.

Partial Intershelving of Microcomputer Disks

Hanging Devices. Hanging bags can house both disks and accompanying documentation (see Figure 9). Before placing 5¼-inch disks in the bags, they should be enclosed in rigid protective containers.

A general description of hanging bags is found in Chapter 4.

References

1. Beatrice Kovacs, "Preservation of Materials in Science and Technology Libraries," *Science and Technology Libraries*, vol. 7, no. 3 (Spring 1987): 7. Nancy B. Olson, "Hanging Your Software Up to Dry," *College & Research Library News*, vol. 47, no. 10 (November 1986): 634–36. Larry N. Osborne "Those (In)Destructible Disks; or, Another Myth Exploded," *Library Hi Tech*, vol. 7, no. 3 (1989): 3–7, 28.

2. Jean Polly, "Circulating Software: Some Sensible Groundrules," *Wilson Library Bulletin*, vol. 60, no. 10 (June 1986): 22.

Further Reading

Adcock, Donald C. *Guidelines for Cataloging Microcomputer Software*. Chicago: American Library Association, 1987.

> The cataloging rules are out-of-date; however, there are three pages of text and illustrations about storage containers.

Anderson, Lou, et al. "Handling Printed Materials with Accompanying Computer Disks." *Computers in Libraries*. 10 (4) (April 1990): 23–25.

> A synopsis of a university library's task force on the handling of disk-accompanied printed materials acquired in a library without a computer facility.

Beaubien, Denise M., et al. "Patron-Use Software in Academic Library Collections." *College & Research Libraries News*. 49 (10) (November 1988): 661–67.
> The questions posed by, and excerpts from the recommendations of, the University of Florida Libraries' Software Study Committee include access and preservation issues.

Brennan, Patricia B.M., and Silverberg, Joel S. "Will My Disks Go Floo If I Take Them Through?" *College & Research Libraries News*. 46 (8) (September 1985): 423–24.
> "A series of experiments ... designed to determine the effect of a magnetic security system (Tattle Tape model #31) on a standard 5[¼]-inch minifloppy disk."

Char, Carlene. "A Complete Guide to the Disk." In *Microcomputer Information for School Media Centers*, edited by Nevada Wallis Thomason, pp. 165–78. Metuchen, NJ: Scarecrow, 1985.
> A basic guide to the construction and care of 5¼-inch disks.

"Circulating Software: A Report from Minneapolis Public Library." *Technicalities*. 5 (2) (February 1985): 15.
> Briefly discusses the packaging and handling of microcomputer software for circulation and reports that "the most remarkable aspect ... has been the lack of problems."

Cohen, Doreen. "The Software Library." *Small Computers in Libraries*. 5 (9) (October 1985): 26–27.
> Describes the care, handling, and storage of microcomputer software in a California Public Library.

Dewey, Patrick R., and Garber, Marvin. "Organizing and Storing Diskettes." *School Library Journal*. 30 (8) (April 1984): 32.

Doll, Carol A. "The Care and Handling of Micro Disks." *School Library Journal*. 32 (3) (November 1985): 43.

Grunin, Lori. "Advisor: On or Off?" *PC Magazine*. 9 (15) (September 11, 1990): 27–28.
> A discussion about the controversy over whether and when a microcomputer should be turned on and off.

"Leave It On." *Library Systems Newsletter*. 10 (9) (September 1990): 77.
> A statement that, provided a computer has a good surge protector, it is wise to leave a computer on to avoid damage from fluctuation in the amount of current flowing through it. However, screens should be turned off or down when not in use.

Paskoff, Beth M. "Microcomputer Software in Library Collections." *Library Trends*. 37 (3) (Winter 1989): 302–15.
> Includes a brief review of the care, handling, and storage of microcomputer disks and reports on several libraries' successful circulation with little or no damage to the disks.

Rockman, Ilene. "Microcomputer Circulation in Libraries." *Library Software Review*. 3 (4) (December 1984): 486–96.
> A report on the status of microcomputer-borrowing services offered by public and academic libraries.

Shirinian, George, and Squires, Stan. *Software for the Public*. Richmond Hill, ON: Audio Archives, 1987. Sound cassette.
> A session recorded at the 1987 Ontario Library Association conference in which all aspects of microcomputer disks in public libraries are discussed.

Skinner, Hedley. "Microcomputer Software in Public Libraries." *Audiovisual Librarian*. 13 (4) (November 1987): 200–208.
> Report of a survey of 156 British public libraries concerning loan services for computer software and hardware.

Strauss, Diane. "A Checklist of Issues to be Considered Regarding the Addition of Microcomputer Data Disks to Academic Libraries." *Information Technology and Libraries*. 5 (2) (June 1986): 129–32.

Williams, Gene. "Taking Care of the Small Computer: A Guide for Librarians." *Wilson Library Bulletin*. 61 (4) (December 1986): 14–16.
Some steps to be taken before calling a service technician.

Yerkey, A. Neil. "Machine-Readable Data Files." In *Nonbook Media: Collection Management and User Services*, edited by John W. Ellison and Patricia Ann Coty, pp. 110–27. Chicago: American Library Association, 1987.

Chapter 11
Optical Discs

Optical discs have undergone both retrenchment and advancement in the past few years. Capacitance electronic discs (CEDs), the competitor to the optical disc for the videodisc market, have been withdrawn from the marketplace and optical laser videodiscs with prerecorded movies appear to have lost out to recordable videocassettes for the general consumer dollar, although recently prerecorded optical videodiscs marketed for the general public have reappeared. Optical videodiscs have continued to find a place in educational settings for instructional purposes. They have also been effective as a means of making resources available to a larger public, e.g., over 1600 still images from the National Gallery of Arts together with commentaries and a documentary on the gallery are available on a single videodisc. Videodiscs are an important component of the many interactive multimedia systems (sometimes also called hypermedia or interactive video) that some experts claim will revolutionize our methods of learning and retrieving information.

The digital sound disc, commonly called a compact disc or CD, is the optical format that has had the greatest impact on the public and hence on libraries. Its technology differs from the videodisc in the nature of the signal recorded; the data on a CD are encoded in digital form, on the videodisc in analog form.

Libraries have also acquired CD-ROM (Read Only Memory) discs. Because these are not generally loaned to the public, a specific discussion of their care, handling, and storage is not included in this chapter. Other types of compact discs, such as CD-I (Interactive) and CD-V (Video) discs, which are not yet part of most library collections, are not specifically mentioned although many of the comments in this chapter can be applied to these discs.

Care

The virtues of CDs have been widely announced, and when the CD is compared to the analog sound disc and the analog sound tape, these virtues are impressive: no stylus nor tape head and, therefore, no surface wear; no danger of erasure by magnetic fields; no grooves that harbor dirt; no measurable degradation from continual playing; no attraction for insects; lack of background noise and very low distortion. In addition, CD players are immune to normal shocks and vibrations. These characteristics have led CDs to be labelled "indestructible"; such a description may encourage careless handling. However, optical discs are not impervious to abuse.

While light dust, dirt, fingerprints, and small scratches will not affect signal quality, a large scratch or a large dirt particle, particularly on the blank side of a disc, can obstruct the laser beam. Oils and other corrosive substances will eventually cause deterioration of the protective layers. A sharp object can pierce the label and damage the encoded data beneath the surface layers. It is important, therefore, to keep discs clean and to handle them with reasonable care.

Cleanliness. To retrieve a disc from the "jewel box" in which many are marketed, press a finger on the center spindle, then grasp the edges of the disc with a thumb and a finger and lift out gently without bending the disc. A cracking of the protective lacquer could result from repeated bending. The disc is then held easily without touching its surface by placing a finger in the center hole and a thumb on the edge. Discs should be returned to their containers when not in use. Discs should fit securely on the center spindle to prevent them from becoming loose in their boxes and falling out when the box is opened.

Because circular scratches cause more damage than those crossing a disc's spiral tracks, discs should be cleaned with a dry, lint-free cloth or one moistened with water by wiping them gently from center to edge rather than in the circular motion used to clean analog sound discs. CD cleaning kits and devices are available commercially; avoid those that operate in a circular fashion. Analog sound disc cleaners and solvents should not be used on CD discs.

The laser lens must also be kept clean. Most lens cleaning devices found in CD stores are considered acceptable by media specialists. The lens may be cleaned manually with a cotton swab moistened with lens cleaning fluid. In all cases, the equipment's manual should be read before any lens cleaning is attempted.

Scratches. It is impossible to repair some scratched discs. *Consumer Reports* describes rescuing "one deeply scratched CD by polishing it with a cotton swab and silver polish".[1] Two years later the *Consumer Reports* staff experimented with several products: Data Mud, Rally cream auto wax, a silver polish, an acrylic floor wax, and a glass polish.

> Nothing worked on severe scratches. But both the *Mud* and the *Rally* wax dramatically reduced the number of errors caused by light scratches. We were even able to restore one unplayable CD to playable condition.[2]

However, car wax should not be used to clean undamaged discs because it will cause eventual deterioration of the protective layers.

Heat and Humidity. Prolonged exposure to direct sunlight, heat, or humidity may damage optical discs. Humidity can cause oxidation of the recording surface and heat can accelerate this process. Like analog sound discs, laser optical discs can be damaged when left in cars on a sunny day.

Labels. Experts express caution about affixing labels to discs because a label can affect the balance resulting in distortion and the label's adhesive may be damaging to the disc. Labels can also become stuck in playback equipment causing havoc. They suggest that labels, bar codes, etc., should be placed on the jewel box or case. If a library wishes to have its identification on a disc, it should be placed as close to the hub as possible because there are no data underneath the protective layers in this area. Some libraries use a stylus for this purpose. The staff of the National Archives of Canada recommends a very fine permanent felt tip marker. Etching is to be avoided because it might serve as a trap for dirt.

Storage

CDs in their jewel boxes or cases can be stored horizontally or vertically. Vertical storage is best for intershelving because it consumes less space. Horizontal storage is an option in partial intershelving.

All of the methods for storing analog sound discs described in Chapter 5 can be used for videodiscs. However, videodiscs have a heavier weight than analog sound discs. Heavy duty shelving must be used in areas where many videodiscs and/or analog sound discs are to be housed. If a library does not have heavy duty shelving, it must limit the number of discs to be placed on any one shelf or, possibly, section of shelving.

Intershelving of Optical Discs

Boxes and Pamphlet Boxes. Many CDs are received in one of two types of clear plastic containers, jewel boxes or compact disc cases, both designed with a center spindle that holds the disc in place and prevents lateral pressure by keeping it away from the surface of the container. Jewel boxes are made of rigid plastic and designed so that the CD sits in a well. CD cases have small retaining ridges rather than a well and the plastic is less rigid. There have been some complaints about their fragility without an indication that one type is preferred to the other. Personal examination indicates that jewel boxes provide more protection. Undoubtedly in response to the fragility complaints, suppliers' catalogs claim their "replacement" containers to be "indestructible." Time will tell. Some containers have a device that automatically unlocks and lifts the disc when opened for ease in handling. CD cases and jewel boxes are easily intershelved.

Sets comprised of more than one disc can be housed in jewel boxes that snap together (up to four discs) or in boxes made of box-board (designed to hold up to three discs) or of pressboard (designed to hold up to four discs). General use pamphlet boxes and Princeton files can also accommodate multipart sets (see Figure 35e).

A general discussion about boxes is found in Chapter 4.

Book-like Albums. There are reasons why a library may wish to house a disc in its jewel box or case in a larger container: the fear that intershelved discs may be pushed out of sight among larger materials; dissatisfaction with flimsy jewel boxes or cases; the presence of accompanying materials that cannot be accommodated in jewel boxes and cases. Several types of albums are available, designed either to house boxes/cases only or boxes/cases and accompanying materials (see Figures 34b and 38).

A general description of book-like albums is found in Chapter 4.

Binders. Binders also answer the need for a larger storage container and may be used for multipart items as well (see Figure 35b). Sleeve pages that hold CDs can be inserted into pamphlet binders and ring binders together with accompanying textual materials.

A general description of binders is found in Chapter 4.

Figure 38. Optical disc and accompanying printed material in book-like album.

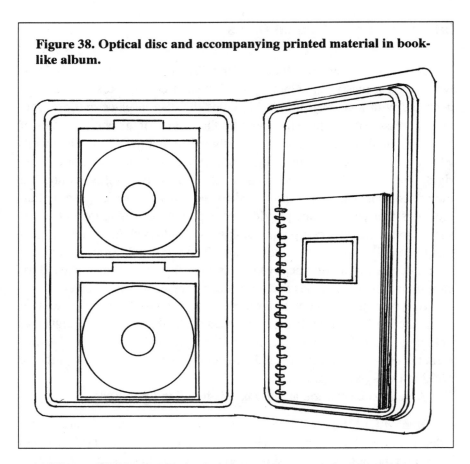

Clip-on Holders. CDs in their boxes/cases may be housed in narrow clip-on holders, which give them additional support and hold them at the front of a shelf. Large holders can accommodate multidisc sets and videodiscs.

A general description of clip-on holders is found in Chapter 4.

Modular Units. Modular units similar to the ones described for analog sound tapes on page 58 are available for CDs.

Partial Intershelving of Optical Discs

Hanging Devices. Hanging bags can accommodate CDs in their boxes/cases, videodiscs, and accompanying materials (see Figure 9).

A general description of hanging devices is found in Chapter 4.

Multimedia Shelf with Adjustable Spacing Panels. CDs and video-discs can be housed in the compartments described and illustrated on page 44. Some devices, such as the add-a-file with interlocking units, can be used for CDs because of their small size.

Multimedia Shelf with Pull-Out Rack or Bin. Videodiscs can be housed in the bins or racks described on page 44 and illustrated on page 45. Similar units are available commercially for CDs.

Multimedia Shelf with Commercial Racks. The commercial racks described on page 45 and illustrated on page 46 can also be used for videodiscs. Racks sized for CDs are available commercially.

A general discussion about racks is found in Chapter 4.

References

1. "Answers to Basic Questions About CDs," *Consumer Reports*, vol. 50, no. 6 (June 1985): 327.
2. "Wax for Waning CDs," *Consumer Reports*, vol. 52, no. 3 (March 1987): 135.

Further Reading

"CD-ROM Disc Maintenance and Care." *OLAC Newsletter*. 10 (1) (March 1990): 27–28. Reprinted from *NELINET Newsletter*.

Day, Rebecca. "How to Care for CDs." *Stereo Review*. 55 (2) (February 1990): 66–67.

——————. "Where's the Rot? A Special Report on CD Longevity." *Stereo Review*. 54 (4) (April 1989): 23–24.

The author states that "CD rot" does not occur in discs from well-known CD producers and offers a list of guidelines for proper care and handling.

Dick, Jeff T. "Laserdisc Redux." *Library Journal*. 115 (20) (November 15, 1990): 37–39.

The author recommends that "progressive AV departments need to consider offering" laserdiscs as part of their collection, and includes a few paragraphs on care and handling.

Duchesne, Roddy, and Giesbrecht, Walter W. "CD-ROM: An Introduction." *Canadian Library Journal*. 45 (4) (August 1988): 214–23.

A description, written in nontechnical language, of various types of compact discs, their advantages and disadvantages, and of other optical storage media.

Herther, Nancy K. "CD-ROM Disk Maintenance and Care." *Laserdisk Professional*. 3 (2) (March 1990): 86–87.

Kniesner, John T. "Compact Discs Are a Sound Investment." *Public Libraries*. 26 (2) (Summer 1987): 77–78.

Discusses the care, handling, and storage of CDs.

MacPhee, Joyce. "Consumer Advisor." *Canadian Consumer*. 20 (9) (1990): 47.

Brief points about the care of CDs.

Ridgway, Jim. "Compact Discs—A Revolution in the Making." *Canadian Library Journal.* 43 (1) (February 1986): 23–29.
This overview of digital sound discs includes a chart comparing the digital disc (CD) with the analog sound disc (LP).

Schabert, Daniel R. "Videodiscs." In *Nonbook Media: Collection Management and User Services,* edited by John W. Ellison and Patricia Ann Coty, pp. 349–60. Chicago: American Library Association, 1987.

General Bibliography

General Works

American Library Association. Resources and Technical Services Division. Audiovisual Committee. *"Happiness Is Having One Title."* Chicago: The Committee, [1987].
A pamphlet directed to producers of nonbook materials advocating the consistent labelling of media.

Anderson, Jacqulyn. *How to Process Media.* [2nd ed.] Technical Processes Guide, 1. Nashville, TN: Broadman, 1984.
Includes a simple, step-by-step guide for the accessioning, labelling, and general processing procedures for filmstrips, games, kits, pictures, realia, slides, sound recordings, transparencies, videocassettes, equipment, and vertical files in a small church library.

Birnhack, Juliette. *Audiovisual Resources in a Hospital Library: Their Organization and Management.* London: Mansell, 1987.
A brief overview that includes care, handling, and storage and the pros and cons of shelving systems.

Casciero, Albert J., and Roney, Raymond G. *Audiovisual Technology Primer.* Englewood, CO: Libraries Unlimited, 1988.
This well-illustrated book written in nontechnical language includes descriptions of videorecordings and equipment, slides and equipment, slide mounts, filmstrips, transparencies, motion pictures, and CDs, their processing, cleaning, care and handling with brief comments on storage.

Cassaro, James P., ed. *Planning and Caring for Library Audio Facilities.* MLA Technical Report, 17. Canton, MA: Music Library Association, 1989.
In addition to space planning and equipment, this monograph deals with CDs, videodiscs, videotapes, and DATs.

Ellison, John W. "Non-Book Collections: Storage and Care Practices." *Catholic Library World.* 54 (5) (December 1982): 206–09. Reprinted in *Media Librarianship*, edited by John W. Ellison, pp. 302–16. New York: Neal-Schuman, 1985.
Forms for evaluating care and storage practices in an active collection for film media, magnetic tape, analog sound discs, maps, prints, original paintings, and the general environment.

Evans, Hilary. *Picture Librarianship.* Outline of Modern Librarianship. New York: K.G. Saur, 1980.
Includes the care and handling of prints, engravings, photographs, negatives, and slides in archival and circulating collections; the advantages and disadvantages of mounting; mounting methods; open and closed access.

Harrison, Helen P. ed. *Picture Librarianship.* Phoenix, AZ: Oryx Press, 1981.
Includes essays about the care, handling, and storage of photographs, negatives, illustrations, slides, and to a limited extent, microforms, filmstrips, and transparencies; detailed discussion about mounting techniques and the advantages and disadvantages of mounting. Archival collections are stressed, but some attention is paid to user collections and intershelving.

Hohenstein, Margaret, et al. *Cataloging, Processing, Administering AV Materials: A Model for Wisconsin Schools.* 3rd ed. Madison, WI: Wisconsin Library Association, 1981.
> Includes illustrated directions for processing materials for circulation and brief instructions for the care and intershelving of a wide range of media.

Jonassen, David H. *Nonbook Media: A Self-Paced Instructional Handbook for Teachers and Library Media Personnel.* Hamden, CT: Library Professional Publications, 1982.
> Simple instructions with illustrations and a bibliography for rubber cement mounting and dry mounting on pages 115–23 and film splicing on pages 257–61.

Kemp, Jerrold E., and Dayton, Deane K. *Planning and Producing Instructional Media.* 5th ed. New York: Harper & Row, 1985.
> This basic, well-illustrated text for the audiovisual technician has brief descriptions about handling videotapes and mounting and storing slides.

Library Association of Australia. Audiovisual Services Committee. *Guidelines for Packaging Nonbook Materials.* Sydney: The Association, 1984.
> Provides "guidelines for manufacturers and distributors of nonbook materials for packaging their products making them more suitable as library materials."

Lowry, Marcia Duncan. *Preservation and Conservation in the Small Library.* Small Libraries Publications Series, 15. Chicago: Library Administration and Management Association, American Library Association, 1989.
> Some of the information in this pamphlet directed primarily to book collections is applicable to nonbook materials—workstations, adhesive tapes, torn paper repair, paper cleaning, and water, mold, and mildew prevention and cure. A brief overview of the care and handling of microforms, analog sound discs, and videotapes is included.

McNally, Paul. *Nonbook Materials.* 2nd ed. South Melbourne: Macmillan, 1981.
> Includes chapters on circulation; open and closed access and integrated and segregated shelving; equipment; individual media.

National Research Council. Committee on Preservation of Historical Records. *Preservation of Historical Records.* Washington, DC: National Academy Press, 1986.

Pearse, Linda. *Audio Visual Media for Children in the Public Library.* Library Service to Children, 8. Ottawa: Canadian Library Association, 1987.
> Brief discussions about the storage, care, handling, and equipment requirements for sound recordings, filmstrips, motion pictures, and videocassettes.

Plumbe, Wilfred J. *Tropical Librarianship.* Metuchen, NJ: Scarecrow Press, 1987.

Price, Helen. *Stopping the Rot: A Handbook of Preventive Conservation for Local Studies Collections.* Occasional Paper, 10. Sydney: Library Association of Australia, New South Wales Branch, 1988.
> Includes clearly and concisely written suggestions and instructions, many in bulleted lists, and some illustrations for the care and storage of microforms, sound recordings, film media, videorecordings, and maps; and general prevention and cure techniques.

Research Libraries Group. *RLG Preservation Manual.* 2nd ed. Stanford, CA: RLG, 1986.
> Section 3 is devoted to nonbook materials.

Ritzenthaler, Mary Lynn. *Archives & Manuscripts Conservation: A Manual on Physical Care and Management.* SAA Basic Manual Series. Chicago: Society of American Archivists, 1983.
> Discusses environmental problems, handling, and storage of paper-based materials in archives with some information on microforms, photographic materials, sound recordings, and videotapes. Includes directions for encapsulation and an annotated bibliography.

Root, Nina J. "Preserving and Maintaining Museum Library Collections." In *Museum Librarianship*, edited by John C. Larsen, pp. 51–66. Hamden, CT: Library Professional Publications, 1985.

A discussion of care, handling, storage, security systems, mending, and restoration.

Smith, Merrily A., ed. *Preservation of Library Materials: Conference Held at the National Library of Austria, Vienna, April 7–10, 1986*, sponsored by the Conference of Directors of National Libraries in cooperation with IFLA and UNESCO. IFLA Publications, 40–41. 2 vols. München: K.G. Saur, 1987.

Vol. 2 includes papers on the storage and handling of film media and sound recordings, conservation of paper, pest management, and climate control, and some mention of maps, globes, and works of art.

Sound and Light: Preservation of AV and Microform Materials in Working Collections: [Papers Presented at the] 1984 Annual Conference. [Chicago]: American Library Association, 1984. Sound cassette.

Three speakers discuss the care, handling, and storage of motion pictures, filmstrips, and slides; sound recordings; and microforms.

Swartzberg, Susan G. *Preserving Library Materials: A Manual.* Metuchen, NJ: Scarecrow Press, 1980.

A clearly written, pragmatic overview of the care, handling, and storage of sound recordings, videotapes, art originals, maps, photographs, slides, and microforms.

Vlcek, Charles W., and Wiman, Raymond V. *Managing Media Services: Theory and Practice.* Englewood, CO: Libraries Unlimited, 1989.

Contains a small section devoted to the processing, care, and handling of motion pictures, slides, and videocassettes and their equipment.

Volkman, Herbert. "Preservation." In *A Handbook for Film Archives: Based on the Experiences of Members of the International Federation of Film Archives (FIAF)*, edited by Eileen Bowser and John Kuiper, pp. 13–43. Brussels: FIAF, 1980.

Brief points about the care and handling of magnetic tape with emphasis on environmental conditions and the archival storage of film and magnetic tape.

Wall, Thomas B. "Nonprint Materials: A Definition and Some Practical Considerations on Their Maintenance." *Library Trends.* 34 (1) (Summer 1985): 129–40.

The care of videotapes, motion pictures, sound tapes, slides, transparencies, and filmstrips is discussed in connection with environmental concerns, magnetic fields, security measures, and circulation policies. Brief attention is given to handling and storage.

Weihs, Jean, with assistance from Lewis, Shirley. *Nonbook Materials: The Organization of Integrated Collections.* 3rd ed. Ottawa: Canadian Library Association, 1989.

Pages 121–25 give concise, general descriptions of the care and handling of analog sound discs, film media, magnetic tape, microscope slides, optical discs, two- and three-dimensional materials with suggestions for intershelving and partial intershelving.

General Bibliographies

Baxter, Paula A. *International Bibliography of Art Librarianship: An Annotated Compilation.* IFLA Publications, 37. München: K.G. Saur, 1987.

Includes some citations on the care, handling, and storage of original art, microforms, photographs, slides, pictures, video and audio media.

Chickering, William F. *Preservation of Nonprint Materials in Working Collections: A Basic Bibliography.* SOLINET Preservation Program Leaflet, 3. Atlanta, GA: Southern Library Network, 1985.
Citations "offer ways of extending the useful life of nonprint materials in collections that are available to the public."

Cloonan, Michele V. "The Preservation of Library Materials and Art on Paper." *Conservation Administration News.* 18 (July 1984): 6, 8.
Publications available from the Library of Congress, the Smithsonian Institution, the U.S. Department of Agriculture, the National Bureau of Standards, and UNESCO.

Collister, Edward A. *The Preservation and Restoration of Library Materials: A Basic and Practical Reading List.* Architecture Series: Bibliography, A1456. Monticello, IL: Vance Bibliographies, 1985.
The citations are listed in broad subject groupings that include environmental factors and the preservation of microforms, photographs, sound recordings, maps, and paper.

Daniel, Evelyn H., and Notowitz, Carol I. *Media and Microcomputers in the Library: A Selected, Annotated Resource Guide.* Phoenix, AZ: Oryx Press, 1984.
Among these 579 citations, arranged in broad subject categories, are 16 devoted to storage and care. A directory of producers, distributors, and publishers includes U.S. and a few British, Canadian, and New Zealand firms.

Ericson, Timothy L.; with the assistance of Ebben, Linda; and Risteen, Deborah. *Audiovisuals for Archivists.* Chicago: Society of American Archivists, 1982.
This annotated bibliography oriented to the archival conservation of books contains citations of use to nonbook collections, such as equipment required, price and/or loan details, and contact organizations.

Fox, Lisa L. *A Core Collection in Preservation*, compiled for the Education Committee of the Preservation of Library Materials Section, Resources and Technical Services Division, American Library Association. Chicago: RTSD, 1988.
Some of the citations deal with the environment and nonbook materials.

Library of Congress. Preservation Office. *Audiovisual Resources for Preserving Library and Archival Materials.* Preservation Leaflet, 6. Washington, DC: Preservation Office, 1983. Free.
A list of audiovisual materials about conservation that can be borrowed by U.S. institutions from the Preservation Office.

Library of Congress. National Preservation Office. *Fact Sheet: Magnetic Media Preservation: Selected Bibliography.* Preservation Information Series: Associations, Agencies, and Resources. Washington, DC: Library of Congress, 1988. Typescript. Free.
Includes magnetic tapes, disks, sound recordings, and motion pictures.

Library of Congress. National Preservation Office. *Fact Sheet: Motion Picture Preservation 1970–1989: Selected Bibliography.* Preservation Information Series: Associations, Agencies, and Resources. Washington, DC: Library of Congress, 1989. Typescript. Free.
While most citations are for the archival preservation of motion picture film, a few have a broader focus and a couple deal with microfilm and video.

Liebscher, Peter. *Audiovisual Librarianship: A Select Bibliography, 1965–1983.* [London]: Audiovisual Librarian, Aslib & Library Association Audiovisual Groups, 1984.
This list of approximately 1700 citations, a few with annotations, includes works on preservation, storage, and multimedia collections.

Saretzky, Gary. "Bibliographies and Databases on the Preservation of Aural and Graphic Records." *Picturescope*. 31 (4) (Winter 1985): 119–21.

West Bengal (India). National Library. *Conservation of Library Materials: A Select Reading List*. Calcutta: The Library, 1985.
This bibliography, which covers many media, is divided into four sections: bibliographies, books, articles, and Indian Standards Institution publications. It includes items published in the 20th century and a few from the 19th century.

General Directories

AV Market Place. New York: Bowker. Annual.
A list of producers, distributors, production companies, and production services for audiovisual materials, equipment manufacturers, distributors, and dealers; with other helpful information.

Coleman, Christopher D.G. *Preservation Education Directory*. 6th ed. Chicago: Association for Library Collections & Technical Services, 1990.
Compiled for the Preservation of Library Materials Section's Education Committee, this booklet lists the preservation and conservation programs and courses offered by universities and other institutions in the U.S. and Canada, and has some information about activities in other countries.

The Equipment Directory of Audio-Visual, Computer and Video Products. Fairfax, VA: NAVA, International Communications Industries Association. Annual.
Although devoted to equipment, this directory has some pictures and technical specifications for cabinets and shelving.

Index to Canadian Library Supplies. [4th ed.] Toronto: Libraries and Community Information Branch, Ontario Ministry of Citizenship and Culture, 1985.
This booklet has a bilingual list of products keyed to an alphabetic list of Canadian suppliers.

International Micrographics Source Book, Including Related Imaging Technologies. Larchmont, N.Y.: Microfilm Publishing. Annual.
Extensive information about micrographics and optical digital data discs.

"Library Journal Sourcebook." *Library Journal*.
This list of products and services keyed to a list of suppliers is published annually in one issue between September and November. (In 1990 it was the October 23 issue, vol. 115, no. 18)

Museum & Archival Supplies Handbook. 3rd ed. rev. and expanded. Toronto: Ontario Museum Association & Toronto Area Archivists Group, 1985.
A list of products with brief descriptions and suggested suppliers arranged in subject groupings. Although the book concentrates on sources used by institutions in Canada and the northeastern U.S., branches elsewhere are given. Includes a bibliography, index, and some illustrations.

Sound Recordings

Almquist, Sharon G. *Sound Recordings in the Library*. University of Illinois Graduate School of Library and Information Science Occasional Papers, 179. Urbana-Champaign: University of Illinois Graduate School of Library and Information Science, 1987.
This history of the development of sound recordings and their place in library collections contains some brief discussions about their care, handling, and storage.

Harrison, Helen, with a contribution from Schuursma, Rolf L. *The Archival Appraisal of Sound Recordings and Related Materials: A RAMP Study with Guidelines*. Paris: UNESCO, 1987.

Hoffman, Frank W. *The Development of Library Collections of Sound Recordings.* Books in Library and Information Science. New York: Dekker, 1979.
Pages 80–90 contain a good discussion of cleaning methods and products; pros and cons of open access; and problems of ensuring proper care while an item is in circulation.

McWilliams, Jerry. *The Preservation and Restoration of Sound Recordings.* Nashville: American Association for State and Local History, 1979.
A thorough description of the care, handling, storage, and restoration of analog sound discs, tapes, cylinders, wires, and digital recordings in archival collections. Includes an annotated bibliography.

Roth, Stacey. "The Care and Preservation of Sound Recordings." *Conservation Administration News.* 23 (October 1985): 4–5, 24.
Analog and digital sound discs, magnetic tape, and wax cylinders are discussed.

Schuller, Dietrich. "Handling, Storage and Preservation of Sound Recordings Under Tropical and Subtropical Climatic Conditions." In *Vital Arts, Vital Libraries: Cultural Life and Tradition in Developing Countries and the Role of Libraries: Papers from the IFLA Conference at Nairobi, August 1984,* pp. 92–101. [S.l.]: IFLA Section of Art Libraries with the IFLA Round Table on Audiovisual Media, 1985. Also published in *Fontis Artis Musicae.* 33 (1) (Januar-Marz 1986): 100–104.
A discussion of the environmental conditions and microorganisms affecting vinyl discs and magnetic tapes.

Magnetic Media

DeWhitt, Benjamin L. "Long-Term Preservation of Data on Computer Magnetic Media." *Conservation Administration News.* 29 (April 1987): 7, 19, 28, 30 (July 1987): 4, 24.
Most of this article is devoted to computer magnetic tapes with a short addendum on microcomputer disks. Much of the material can be applied to magnetic tapes in general.

Geller, Sidney B. *Care and Handling of Computer Magnetic Storage Media.* Computer Science and Technology. Washington, DC: National Bureau of Standards, U.S. Department of Commerce, 1983.
Handling methods and environmental conditions in daily and long-term archival storage for computer tapes and disks are presented in bulleted lists in this definitive technical report.

Art Originals

Ellis, Margaret Holben. *The Care of Prints and Drawings.* Nashville: American Association for State and Local History, 1987.
Included are discussions of basic conservation procedures, storage, and environmental conditions.

Foster, Donald L. "Original Art." In *Nonbook Media: Collection Management and User Services,* edited by John W. Ellison and Patricia Ann Coty, pp. 193–213. Chicago: American Library Association, 1987.

O'Reilly, Priscilla. *Paintings.* Preservation Guide, 3. New Orleans: Historic New Orleans Collection, 1986.
Environmental conditions, handling, and potential problems are discussed.

Rosenbaum, Lee. *The Complete Guide to Collecting Art.* New York: Knopf, 1982.
One chapter deals with the care, handling, and storage of works of art.

Simmons, Rosemary. *Collecting Original Prints.* Christie's International Collectors Series. New York: Mayflower Books, 1980.
One chapter in this book for the amateur collector is devoted to framing and conservation.

Warner, Glen. *Building a Print Collection: A Guide to Buying Original Prints and Photographs.* Toronto: Key Porter Books, 1984.
Pages 159–74 have a well-illustrated discussion about the care, mounting, framing, handling, storage, and hanging of original prints and photographs.

Photographs

Albright, Gary. "Which Envelope? Selecting Storage Enclosures for Photographs." *Picturescope.* 31 (4) (Winter 1985): 111–13.
A clearly written discussion about the advantages, disadvantages, and special precautions involved in various types of enclosures.

Conservation of Photographs. Rochester, NY: Eastman Kodak, 1985.
A detailed description of the preservation, restoration, and storage of photographs for the conservator and the individual collector.

DeCandido, Robert. "Out of the Question." *Conservation Administration News.* 21 (April 1985): 3, 21.
Discusses the best storage enclosures for photographs when a library has a limited budget.

DiFelice, Clara L. "Photographs." In *Nonbook Media: Collection Management and User Services,* edited by John W. Ellison and Patricia Ann Coty, pp. 262–73. Chicago: American Library Association, 1987.

Kennedy, Nora, and Mustardo, Peter. "Current Issues in the Preservation of Photographs." *AB Bookman's Weekly.* 83 (17) (April 24, 1989): 1773–1783.
Buffered vs nonbuffered enclosures, light levels during exhibitions, and chemical restorative treatments are discussed.

Lawrence, John H. *Photographs.* Preservation Guide, 2. New Orleans: Historic New Orleans Collection, 1983. Excerpts are published in *LAA Bulletin.* 49 (1) (Summer 1986): 27–30.
Includes a discussion of enclosures, handling, and some storage.

Orcutt, Joyce. "The Care and Preservation of Photographic Materials." *AB Bookman's Weekly.* 80 (16) (November 2, 1987): 1681, 1684, 1686, 1688–1689.
A discussion of environment, pollutants, and storage for photograph archives.

Polaroid Corporation. *Storing, Handling and Preserving Polaroid Photographs: A Guide.* Boston: Focal Press, [19--].
Includes appropriate environmental conditions, protection from physical damage, storage of photographs and negatives, methods of mounting and framing.

Reilly, James M., et al. "Photographic Enclosures: Research and Specifications." *Restaurator.* 10 (3/4) (1989): 102–111.
The harmful effects on photographs of materials used in storage enclosures, methods for evaluating enclosures, and practical guidelines for choosing enclosures are described.

Rempel, Siegfried. *The Care of Photographs.* New York: Nick Lyons Books, 1987.
Written in nontechnical English this illustrated book includes information on the care, handling, and storage of photographs.

Ritzenthaler, Mary Lynn; Munoff, Gerald J.; and Long, Margery S. *Archives & Manuscripts: Administration of Photographic Collections.* SAA Basic Manual Series. Chicago: Society of American Archivists, 1984.
A thorough, practical discussion of all aspects of photographic collections with one chapter on preservation.

Robl, Ernest H. *Organizing Your Photographs.* New York: Amphoto, 1986.
Written in nontechnical language, one chapter has an overview of storage and handling techniques.

Storage Enclosures for Photographic Prints and Negatives. Andover, MA: Northeast Document Conservation Center, 1989. Available free from University Products, Holyoke, MA.

Zucker, Barbara. "Photographs: Their Care and Conservation." *Illinois Libraries.* 67 (8) (October 1985): 699–704.
A discussion of the care, handling, and storage of photographs and disaster procedures for all types of film.

Index

by Linda Webster

Italic page numbers refer to figures.